101 Boozy Dessert Recipes
by
Allie Bishop

For Mama Bishop
Who taught me the joy of baking every weekend of my childhood.

TABLE OF CONTENTS

Why Cook With Alcohol?

Alcohol plays a wonderful role in the kitchen. It is used for a number of reasons. To enhance accompanying flavors, to tenderize meat, to infuse flavors, to create light and fluffy baked goods, to stop curdling of certain dishes, as a preservative, and more. Alcohol imparts flavor from the liquid to the dish, conveys aroma from the dish to the nostrils, enhancing flavor, and bonds fat and water molecules, which helps added seasonings to penetrate the dish.

Contrary to popular belief, the alcohol added to a dish does not "burn off" during cooking. A 2003 USDA study showed that between 5% and 85% of alcohol is retained in the dish. The retention of alcohol in a dish is determined by factors such as:

- The volume of alcohol added
- The alcohol percentage of the liquid
- The extent to which the dish is heated
- The length of time the dish is cooked
- The style and surface area of cookware employed

Because of this, it is always advisable to inform your guests that there is alcohol used in the dish. Allergies, health problems, addictions and medications can have compounding issues. If you are aware of any issues your guests may have with alcohol, smaller amounts of alcohol can be exchanged for extract, juices or concentrates. Recipes with larger amounts of alcohol will be altered too dramatically with an exchange, so are best avoided altogether.

The old adage "never cook with wine you wouldn't drink" is often applied to the use of all alcohol in the kitchen. However, there is a lot of debate over this. Many professional chefs agree that, in practice, the quality of the alcohol used, while sometimes causing subtle changes in the nuances of the flavor, doesn't really change the quality of the dish. That said, never cook with alcohol that isn't drinkable at all, for example cooking wine. Most recipes can be altered to taste, in regards to the amount of alcohol added and to the brand used. Though, for frozen desserts you will want to be accurate with your measurements, as too much alcohol can stop the dish from freezing.

Wine

Wine has long been used as an accompaniment to food. A glass of wine paired with the right dish enhances the flavor of both the dish and the wine. It is also the most common alcohol to be added to dishes. In regards to sweet dishes, red wine is commonly paired with chocolate, while dessert wines are used to add sweetness. Red wines enhance flavors with a more robust nature, while white wines enhance lighter dishes.

Dishes that call for water can often be exchanged for wine - the measurements are the same, and it will add a twist to the flavor. Non-alcoholic wines can be used to substitute if you wish to reduce the amount of alcohol. But be aware, non-alcoholic wines still contain trace amounts of alcohol, which can interfere with medications.

Never cook with wine labeled "cooking wine". This contains a large array of salt, additives, preservatives and sulphites and is not at all drinkable, so it is not edible either.

Blackberry Merlot Granita

Serves 8

Ingredients:

2 cups Merlot	1/2 cup sugar, or to taste
6 cups blackberries	1 teaspoon lemon juice

Method:

1. Boil cabernet over a medium heat. Reduce heat and simmer until liquid has reduced by half.

2. Refrigerate for 1 hour.

3. Purée and strain blackberries and lemon juice.

4. Whisk together wine, sugar and blackberry mixture until sugar dissolves.

5. Either use your icecream maker as per manufacturer's instructions, or place in freezer, stirring vigorously every 30 minutes.

Merlot Brownies

Serves 16

Ingredients:

1/2 cup butter

1/2 cup unsweetened cocoa powder

1 cup sugar

3 eggs

1 teaspoon vanilla extract

1/2 cup Merlot

1/2 cup plus 1 tablespoon all-purpose flour

1/4 teaspoon salt

4oz (113g) cream cheese

1/2 cup confectioners' sugar

Method:

1. Preheat oven to 350 °F (175 °C).

2. Melt butter and mix with cocoa powder, sugar, 2 eggs, vanilla,

3. Merlot, flour, and salt until just incorporated.

4. In a separate bowl, blend cream cheese, confectioners' sugar, and remaining egg.

5. Pour half of the brownie batter into the pan, spread cream cheese mixture on top, then pour remaining brownie batter on top of the cream cheese mixture.

6. Bake for 30-35 minutes or until done.

Strawberries with Black Pepper Cabernet Syrup

Serves 4

Ingredients:

1 cup sugar

1 cup cabernet sauvignon

1 teaspoon salt

1 teaspoon black pepper, freshly ground

1 teaspoon balsamic vinegar

2 pints fresh berries

Method:

1. Bring sugar and wine to a boil, stirring occasionally until sugar dissolves.

2. Once boiling, stop stirring and continue to boil until thick and syrupy.

3. Remove from heat, and stir in black pepper and balsamic vinegar.

4. Allow to cool and pour over berries.

Frozen Blueberry Cabernet Cheesecake

Serves 8

Ingredients:

1 pint of blueberries

1/2 cup cabernet sauvignon

1/2 cup sugar dissolved in 1/2 cup boiling water

1/4 cup heavy cream

1/4 cup cream cheese

4 tablespoons of sugar

1/4 cup graham cracker crumbs

Method:

1. Puree blueberries, wine and sugar dissolved in boiling water. Set aside.

2. Beat cream cheese until light and fluffy. Set aside.

3. Beat cream and sugar until soft peaks form.

4. Fold cream cheese into cream and sugar.

5. Place 1/4 cup of mixture into a bowl and whisk in graham cracker crumbs.

6. Into small bowls or popsicle molds, pour 2 tablespoons of blueberry mixture. Spread a tablespoon of cheesecake mixture on top of blueberry layer. Spread a teaspoon, of graham cracker mixture on top of cheesecake mixture. Continue layering until top of bowl or mold is reached.

7. Freeze.

Strawberry Marsala Zabaglione

Serves 2

Ingredients:

10-12 fresh strawberries, thinly sliced

2 large egg yolks

2 tablespoons sugar

2 tablespoons sweet Marsala wine

Method:

1. Whisk together egg yolks, sugar, and Marsala wine in a heatproof bowl and place bowl over a saucepan filled with 1-2 inches of simmering water.

2. Whisk until doubled in volume.

3. Spoon over sliced berries.

Cabernet Truffles

Serves 30

Ingredients:

3/4 cup heavy cream

5oz (140g) milk chocolate, chopped

5oz (140g) dark chocolate, chopped

3 tablespoons cabernet sauvignon

Sprinkles or cocoa powder (for garnish)

Method:

1. Heat cream in a saucepan and as soon as it boils, remove from heat and pour over chocolate.

2. Add wine. Let sit for 3 minutes, then whisk until smooth.

3. Place plastic wrap over top of the chocolate. Refrigerate for 2 hours or more.

4. Roll into balls then coat in cocoa or sprinkles.

5. Refrigerate.

Orange Muscat Gelees with Citrus Fruit

Serves 48

Ingredients:

5 tablespoons cold water

3 packages unflavored gelatin

1/2 cup sugar

1/2 cup water

1 cup orange Muscat or other dessert wine

1 1/4 cups sweet wine

5 pieces mixed citrus fruit

Method:

1. Combine 5 tablespoons cold water and gelatin in a bowl and allow to soften.

2. Combine sugar, 1/2 cup water, and wines in a saucepan and simmer until sugar dissolves. Add gelatin and whisk until dissolved.

3. Remove from heat, and strain into a baking dish. Allow to cool.

4. Peel, pith and segment citrus. Arrange in a single layer over mixture.

5. Refrigerate overnight.

6. Invert onto a serving plate.

Muscat Peach Melba

Serves 8

Ingredients:

2 cups Muscat or other dessert wine

1 1/2 teaspoons vanilla extract

4 large ripe peaches, halved and pitted

1/2 cup sugar

2 pints raspberry sorbet

Raspberries (for garnish)

Method:

1. Mix wine, vanilla-bean seeds, vanilla extract and peaches, and leave to marinate 2 hours, occasionally spooning marinade over peaches.

2. Transfer peaches to a flat plate and refrigerate.

3. Bring marinade and sugar to a boil until reduced by half.

4. Place peaches into dessert bowls, put a spoonful of sorbet into the dip and drizzle with syrup.

Muscat Crème Brûlée

Serves 6

Ingredients:

Custard:

2 1/2 cups whipping cream

3/4 cup sugar

1/2 cup Muscat or other dessert wine

2 tablespoons lemon juice

Brûlée:

1/4 cup maple syrup

3 tablespoons rolled oats

1 1/2 cups mixed fresh berries

Method:

Custard:

1. Heat the cream and sugar until sugar dissolves.

2. Remove from heat and stir in Muscat and lemon juice.

3. Allow to cool, and pour into dessert bowls. Refrigerate overnight.

5. Arrange berries over custard and arrange broken shards of brûlée over berries.

Brûlée

1. Preheat oven to 375 °F (190 °C).

2. Mix together maple syrup and oats until oats fully coated.

3. Pour into a lightly greased pan, and spread evenly.

4. Bake for 15 to 20 minutes, or until done.

5. Allow to cool.

Champagne

Champagne was first created by the monk Dom Perignon, who reportedly cried "Oh, come quickly, I am drinking stars!" While true champagne comes from the region of Champagne in Northeast France, it has come to be used interchangeably with the terms spumante, sparkling wine, or, colloquially, "bubbles". It has become a symbol for celebration, imbibed on such occasions as New Year's Eve, weddings, births, job promotions, graduation.... basically any time you want to celebrate.

Once opened, a champagne stopper will keep the champagne fresh for a couple of days, but after that, why not use it in your cooking? Champagne can be used in place of white wine (and vice versa) in cooking, and specifically lends itself well to baking, with the bubble lifting and lightening breads, cakes, scones, muffins and more. If you want a non-alcoholic version, soda can be substituted.

Grapefruit Pomegranate Champagne Sorbet

Serves 8

Ingredients:

2 1/2 cup grapefruit juice, freshly squeezed, strained

1/2 cup pomegranate juice, freshly squeezed, strained

1/2 cup + 2 tablespoons sugar

1/2 cup champagne

2 tablespoons lemon juice, freshly squeezed, strained

Method:

1. Squeeze and strain grapefruits.

2. Squeeze and strain pomegranate seeds.

3. Stir 1 cup of grapefruit juice with sugar over a medium heat until sugar dissolves.

4. Remove from heat, and add remaining juices and champagne.

5. Refrigerate until thoroughly cool.

6. Either use your icecream maker as per manufacturer's instructions, or place in freezer, stirring vigorously every 30 minutes.

Champagne Pomegranate Jelly

Serves 8

Ingredients:

1 bottle pink champagne   9 leaves of gelatine

18oz (500g) caster sugar   Seeds of 3 pomegranates

Method:

1. Heat champagne and sugar, but do not allow to boil .

2. Add the softened gelatine, take off the heat and stir until dissolved.

3. Pour an inch of the mixture into champagne flutes, and refrigerate to set.

4. Add a layer of pomegranate seeds and a teaspoon of champagne mix to set them in place. Refrigerate to set.

5. Repeat last 2 steps until mixture is used.

Beer

Beer has been used in cooking for thousands of years. The hops and barley add to a recipe the way spices do, and beer is used to enhance and enrich baking. Even for those who don't like the taste of beer, when used in baking it can magnify the flavor. The yeast in beer makes the baked goods lighter and spongier.

Beer in baking isn't just for the boys. Guinness, in particular, goes well with chocolate and strawberries (and I think we can agree chocolate and strawberries are for everyone!). Guinness is the beer most often used in baking sweet treats as it complements the flavor of food very well. However, it can be substituted for any stout or dark beer. To make measurements for Guinness, pour and let settle before measuring.

With the multitude of emerging flavors of beer - chocolate, citrus, pumpkin, and more - more and more recipes lend themselves to use with beer.

Creamy Chocolate Guinness

Serves 6

Ingredients:

8 large egg yolks

1 cup sugar

1 can Guinness

3 cups heavy cream

7oz (200g) bittersweet chocolate, finely chopped

Method:

1. Whisk together egg yolks and sugar.

2. Slowly pour Guinness with as little foam as possible.

3. Pour half of Guinness into a saucepan. And whisk in 2 1/4 cups cream.

4. Whisk over a medium heat, until bubbles begin to form at edges.

5. Remove from heat, and stir in chocolate until melted

6. Slowly pour mixture into eggs, whisking constantly.

7. Return to saucepan and whisk over a medium-low heat, until mixture thickens.

8. Blend on high for 1 minute.

9. Pour into serving glasses and refrigerate.

10. Boil remaining Guinness over medium heat, then reduce to medium-low and simmer, until reduced to 1 tablespoon (approximately 20 minutes.)

11. Allow to cool.

12. Beat remaining cream until soft peaks form. Beat in Guinness syrup. Add a dollop to each pudding.

Chocolate Stout Macerated Raspberries

Serves 4

Ingredients:

2 3/4 cups milk

2 3/4 cups heavy cream

1 cup sugar

2 3/4 cups stout

2 pints raspberries

1 tablespoon sugar

Pinch of salt

8oz (225g) dark chocolate, grated (for garnish)

Method:

1. Stir together milk, cream and 1 cup sugar over a medium heat until sugar dissolves.

2. Refrigerate for 2 hours.

3. Whip in stout until foamy.

4. Refrigerate.

5. Puree and strain 1 pint of raspberries with 1 tablespoon sugar and salt.

6. Toss the second pint of raspberries with the puree.

7. Spoon about 1oz (30g) of stout foam onto a plate.

8. Arrange raspberries on the foam.

9. Garnish with chocolate.

Apple Pie with Pale Ale Mascarpone Cream

Serves 8

Ingredients:

Crust:

2 1/2 cups all-purpose flour

1 teaspoon salt

2 tablespoons sugar

12 tablespoons cold unsalted butter, cut into cubes

8 tablespoons vegetable shortening

1/3 cup pale ale

2 tablespoons melted butter

Filling:

3 Honey Crisp apples, peeled, sliced

3 Granny Smith apples, peeled, sliced

1/2 cup brown sugar

1/2 cup white sugar

1/4 cup flour

1 teaspoon cinnamon

1/4 teaspoon nutmeg

1 tablespoon lemon juice

1 tablespoon pale ale

Cream:

8oz (225g) mascarpone

1 cup powdered sugar

1 teaspoon vanilla extract

1/4 cup pale ale

Method:

Crust:

1. Blend 1 1/2 cups of flour, salt and sugar in a food processor. Add butter and shortening, and blend until well combined.

2. Add remaining flour and blend briefly.

3. Stir together beer and dough.

4. Divide the dough evenly and form into flat disks.

5. Wrap each disk in plastic wrap, and refrigerate 1 hour.

Filling:

1. Place apples in a bowl and sprinkle with brown sugar, flour, cinnamon, nutmeg, lemon juice and beer. Toss until coated.

2. Roll out one of the pastry disks out on a lightly floured surface and line a 9-inch pie pan.

3. Pour the filling into the base.

4. Roll out the remaining dough, cut shapes with a small cookie cutter and layer over the filling.

5. Brush with melted butter, sprinkle with sugar.

6. Place pie in the freezer for ten minutes while the oven preheats.

7. Preheat oven to 350 °F (175 °C).

8. Bake for 40 minutes or until done.

9. To serve: combine mascarpone, powdered sugar, vanilla and pale ale and use to top pie.

Pale Ale Meringues

Serves 16

Ingredients:

3 large egg whites

Pinch of salt

1/3 cup granulated sugar

1/2 cup powdered sugar

3 tablespoons pale ale

Method:

1. Preheat oven to 200 °F (90 °C).

2. Beat egg whites and salt until light and frothy. Very gradually add granulated sugar, beat until peaks form.

3. Add powdered sugar and beer, beat until peaks return.

4. Spoon or pipe meringue onto a baking sheet lined with wax paper.

5. Bake 2 hours, or until dry.

Cream Cheese Caramel Ale Pumpkin Pie

Serves 8

Ingredients:

Filling:
16oz (450g) cream cheese, softened

2/3 cup brown sugar

1/2 cup white sugar

1/2 teaspoon cinnamon

1/4 teaspoon nutmeg

1/4 teaspoon salt

1/2 teaspoon vanilla extract

1/4 cup brown ale beer (barley wine will also be great)

15oz (425g) pumpkin puree

2/3 cup caramel sauce

1/2 cup candied pecans

Crust:
9 graham crackers

3 tablespoons brown sugar

7 tablespoons melted butter

Method:
1. Blend graham crackers, brown sugar and melted butter in a food processor.
2. Press into the bottom of a 9 inch pan.
3. Beat cream cheese, brown sugar and white until light and fluffy.
4. Add the cinnamon, nutmeg, salt, vanilla extract, beer, and pumpkin puree and beat until well combined.
5. Spread filling evenly in the base.
6. Top with caramel sauce and candied pecans.
7. Refrigerate.

Porter-Infused Chocolate Mousse Tart with Potato Chip Crust

Serves 8

Ingredients:

1 bag potato chips

1/2 cup flour

3 tablespoons cornstarch

2 tablespoons brown sugar

3 tablespoons melted butter

10oz (280g) dark chocolate chips

1/2 cup + 2 tablespoons porter

2 cups heavy cream

1/3 cup powdered sugar

1/4 teaspoon salt

Method:

1. Preheat oven to 350 °F (175 °C).

2. Crumb chips, flour, cornstarch, and brown sugar in a food processor.

3. Add the melted butter and process until well combined.

4. Press into a 9-inch tart pan.

5. Bake for 10-12 minutes, or done.

6. Combine the chocolate chips and 1/2 cup porter in a microwave-proof bowl. Microwave for 45 seconds, stir and repeat until melted. Allow to cool.

7. Beat together cream, remaining porter, salt and powdered sugar until peaks form.

8. Gradually add chocolate until well combined.

9. Spread evenly into base.

10. Refrigerate until ready to serve.

Chocolate Stout Caramel Tart

Serves 8

Ingredients:

Crust:

3 1/2 cups mini pretzels

2 tablespoons brown sugar

8 tablespoons melted butter

Caramel Layer:

2 cups white sugar

12 tablespoons unsalted butter, cubed

1/3 cup heavy cream

1/4 cup chocolate stout

Chocolate Layer:

10oz (280g) dark chocolate

1/3 cup chocolate stout

3 tablespoons heavy cream

Method:

1. Preheat oven to 350 °F (175 °C).

2. Crumb pretzels and brown sugar in a food processor.

3. Add melted butter, and blend until well combined.

4. Press firmly into the bottom of a 9-inch tart pan.

5. Bake for 12 minutes or until done.

6. In the top of a double boiler combine chocolate, stout, and cream and stir until melted.

7. Pour filling into base.

8. Refrigerator until set.

9. Place sugar in a saucepan, stirring constantly until melted. Once melted, stop stirring and allow to boil.

10. Remove from heat and immediately stir in butter, cream and stout.

11. Allow to cool for 15 minutes then pour over chocolate layer.

12. Refrigerate until set.

Frangelico

Frangelico is the most well-known hazelnut liqueur. It is a versatile liqueur in baking, bringing a nutty twist to any recipe. Frangelico can be substituted for any hazelnut liqueur, or a nut essence for a non-alcoholic substitute.

Frangelico Granita

Serves 6

Ingredients:

2 cups coffee, freshly brewed

1/2 cup sugar

2 tablespoons Frangelico

Method:

1. Stir together hot coffee and sugar until sugar dissolves.

2. Place over a bowl full of ice water, stirring until chilled.

3. Add Frangelico.

4. Either use your icecream maker as per manufacturer's instructions, or place in freezer, stirring vigorously every 30 minutes.

Frangelico Oreo Icecream

Serves 2

Ingredients:

8fl oz (235ml) whole milk

12fl oz (350ml) heavy cream

2 teaspoons vanilla extract

2 egg yolks

7oz (20g) sugar

1/2 teaspoon salt

1fl oz (30ml) Frangelico

6oz (170g) Oreos (or other mix-in), crushed

Method:

1. Bring milk, cream and vanilla to a simmer.

2. In a bowl, slowly whisk sugar into egg yolk, a little at a time. Whisk in salt.

3. Gradually whisk hot cream into the egg yolks, a little at a time, until egg mixture is quite warm. Transfer back to saucepan and stir over a medium-low heat.

4. Heat until 145° F (62 °C).

5. Strain into a bowl and stir in Frangelico.

6. Either use your icecream maker as per manufacturer's instructions, or place in freezer, stirring vigorously every 30 minutes.

White Chocolate Frangelico Cheesecake

Serves 12

Ingredients:

Cheesecake:

24oz (680g) cream cheese

3/4 cup sugar

8oz (225g) white chocolate, melted

1 teaspoon vanilla

3 tablespoons Frangelico

4 eggs

Crust:

One package chocolate wafers, crumbed

1 stick (113g) butter, melted

Method:

1. Preheat oven to 350 °F (175 °C).

2. Mix together cookie crumbs and melted butter.

3. Press firmly into a 9 inch pan and bake 10 minutes.

5. Decrease oven temperature to 325 °F (160 °C).

6. Beat cream cheese on low for 1 minute then slowly add sugar.

7. Add melted chocolate, vanilla and Frangelico and mix just till combined.

8. Mix in eggs, one at a time, until just incorporated.

9. Pour filling into base.

10. Place pan into a larger pan half filled with water and bake 60 minutes or until set.

11. Allow to cool then refrigerate.

Salted Cinnamon Chilli-Chocolate Frangelico Pudding

Serves 6

Ingredients:

6oz (170g) chopped semi-sweet chocolate

1/4 cup cornstarch

1/2 cup sugar

1/2 teaspoon salt

3 cups whole milk

1 teaspoon cinnamon

1 teaspoon vanilla extract

1 teaspoon instant coffee or espresso powder

1 tablespoon Frangelico

1 teaspoon cayenne

Sea salt (to garnish)

Method:

1. Stir cornstarch, sugar, salt, and milk over a low heat until it thickens. Add the chocolate and stir until melted.

2. Remove from heat and add vanilla, cinnamon, coffee powder, cayenne and Frangelico.

3. Pour into ramekins and refrigerate for 2 hours.

4. Sprinkle sea salt over the top immediately before serving.

Chocolate-Frangelico Crème Anglaise

Serves 8

Ingredients:

2 cups whole milk

1 cup whipping cream

5 large egg yolks

6 tablespoons sugar

4oz (120g) bittersweet chocolate, chopped

5 tablespoons Frangelico

1/2 teaspoon vanilla extract

Method:

1. Bring milk and cream to a simmer.

2. In a bowl, whisk together yolks and sugar.

3. Gradually whisk in hot milk mixture.

4. Return mixture to saucepan and stir over medium-low heat until it thickens.

5. Remove from heat. Add chocolate and whisk until melted. Stir in Frangelico and vanilla.

6. Refrigerate at least 4 hours.

Orange Liqueurs

There are two main styles of orange liqueur - triple sec, a clear grain-based alcohol that gets its name from its triple distillation process, and curaçao, which can most commonly be found colored a bright blue color.

The two big name brands of orange liqueur are Cointreau, a triple sec, and Grand Marnier, a cognac-based orange liqueur.

The rich, complex flavors of both Cointreau and Grand Marnier make them perfect for use in desserts such as pastries and soufflés. Where listed below, Cointreau can be substituted with any triple sec, and Grand Marnier with any brandy-based liqueur. For non-alcoholic alternatives, use either orange essence, orange concentrate, orange juice heated and reduced to a syrup.

Cointreau Sangria Sorbet

Serves 2

Ingredients:

6 tablespoons sugar

2 tablespoons water

2 tablespoons lime juice, freshly squeezed

1/2 cup red wine

2/3 cup orange juice, freshly squeezed

Zest from 1 orange

1 tablespoon Cointreau

Method:

1. In a microwave safe bowl, stir together sugar and water. Heat in the microwave for 1 minute and stir together until sugar is dissolved.

2. Add the remaining Ingredients and stir together well.

3. Cover and refrigerate for four hours or longer.

4. Churn in your ice cream maker. Cover and freeze.

Grand Marnier Strawberry Mousse

Serves 6

Ingredients:

16oz (450g) strawberries

2 tablespoons granulated sugar

1 tablespoons Grand Marnier

1 1/2 cups heavy or whipping cream

2 tablespoons powdered sugar

Lemon zest (for garnish)

Method:

1. Mix together sliced strawberries, granulated sugar and Grand Marnier. Set aside for 30 minutes to marinate.

2. Whip cream and powdered sugar to soft peaks.

3. Puree marinated strawberries and fold into whipped cream.

4. Refrigerate.

5. Garnish with strawberries and lemon zest if desired.

Grand Marnier Crème Brûlée French Toast

Serves 6

Ingredients:

1 loaf unsliced white bread, brioche or rich
bread of your choice

1 1/3 cups whole milk

2/3 cup heavy cream

4 large eggs

1/3 cup granulated sugar

1/4 teaspoon salt

1 teaspoon Grand Marnier

2 teaspoons vanilla extract

2/3 cup granulated sugar

Method:

1. Preheat the oven to 325 °F (160 °C)

2. Cut bread into thick slices, approximately 1 1/2 inches thick.

3. Whisk together milk, cream, eggs, sugar, salt, liqueur, and vanilla extract.

4. Layer bread, single layer, into a large roasting tray.

5. Pour custard over slices. Allow to sit for 15 minutes, turn and allow to sit another 15 minutes.

6. Place slices on a wax paper-lined baking tray.

7. Bake for 30 minutes, turning half way.

8. Melt remaining sugar over a moderate heat, stirring constantly until fully melted.

9. Spread caramel thinly over toast.

10. Allow to cool.

Grand Marnier Drenched Chocolate Strawberries

Serves 16

Ingredients:

16 large strawberries

1/2 cup Grand Marnier

16oz (450g) bittersweet chocolate, chopped

2 tablespoons shortening

2 tablespoons heavy cream

1/4 cup Grand Marnier

1oz (30g) white chocolate, chopped

Method:

1. Using a syringe or marinade injector, inject 2 teaspoons of Grand Marnier into each strawberry and refrigerate for 30 minutes.

2. Over a double boiler, combine bittersweet chocolate and shortening. Stir occasionally until almost melted, then remove from heat and stir until fully melted. Stir in heavy cream and 1/4 cup of Grand Marnier.

3. Over a double boiler, place white chocolate. Stir occasionally until almost melted, then remove from heat and stir until fully melted.

4. Dip strawberries into chocolate, and place on waxed paper to set. Drizzle white chocolate over the top.

Strawberries Romanov

Serves 2

Ingredients:

1/2 cup sour cream

1 1/2 cups vanilla ice cream, softened

1 cup sweetened whipped cream

1/4 cup Cointreau

2 cups fresh strawberries, hulled

2 sprigs mint leaves (for garnish)

Semisweet chocolate, grated (for garnish)

Method:

1. Mix together sour cream, icecream, and whipped cream.

2. Slowly stir in the orange liqueur.

3. Place berries in two parfait glasses, and spoon the cream mixture over them.

4. Garnish with mint leaves and shaved chocolate.

Panettone Pudding with Spiced Cointreau Sauce

Serves 6

Ingredients:

Panettone Pudding:

12oz (340g) panettone, cubed

3 eggs, lightly beaten

1/2 cup white sugar

2 1/4 cups heavy cream

2 teaspoons vanilla extract

1 tablespoon Grand Marnier

Pinch of salt

1/8 teaspoon nutmeg, freshly grated

1 1/2 teaspoons lemon zest, freshly grated

2 teaspoons orange zest, freshly grated

2 1/2 tablespoons unsalted butter, cubed

2 tablespoons white sugar

Sauce:

1/2 cup butter

1 cup white sugar

1/4 cup Grand Marnier

3 tablespoons water

1/8 teaspoon nutmeg, freshly grated

1/8 teaspoon salt

1 egg

Method:

Panettone:

1. Arrange panettone in a casserole dish (not too tightly)

2. Whisk together 3 eggs and 1/2 cup sugar until the sugar is dissolved and the mixture is lemon-colored.

3. Add cream, vanilla, and Grand Marnier and whisk.

4. Stir in salt, 1/8 teaspoon nutmeg, lemon zest, and orange zest.

5. Pour this mixture over panettone.

6. Cover and refrigerate for 30 minutes.

7. Preheat oven to 350 °F (175 °C).

8. Dot the top of the bread pudding with 2 1/2 tablespoons butter, and sprinkle with remaining sugar.

9. Bake 1 hour or until cooked.

10. Spoon sauce over pudding to serve.

Sauce:

1. Melt butter over low heat.

2. Stir in sugar, Grand Marnier, water, nutmeg, and salt and continue to heat over medium heat until the sugar is dissolved and remove from heat.

3. Whisk egg until well beaten. Slowly add to the hot mixture while continuing to whisk.

4. Place the saucepan back over medium-low heat, and stir gently until the sauce almost reaches a simmer. Do not allow to boil. Continue stirring until the sauce thickens, 1 to 2 minutes.

5. Spoon over panettone pudding and serve immediately.

Triple Sec Cheesecake Icecream

Serves 16

Ingredients:

1 quart low-fat 1% milk

16oz (450g) reduced fat cream cheese, softened

1 1/2 cups white sugar

1/3 cup triple sec

1 tablespoon vanilla extract

1 pinch salt

Method:

Blend all ingredients together and either use your icecream maker as per manufacturer's instructions, or place in freezer, stirring vigorously every 30 minutes.

Orange Cups with Cointreau Marmalade Drizzle

Serves 8

Ingredients:

2 tablespoons butter, softened

3/4 cup sugar

1 1/2 teaspoons orange, finely grated zest

1/4 cup orange juice, freshly squeezed

4 eggs, separated

1/4 cup cake flour

4 tablespoons fresh lemon juice

1 cup milk

6 tablespoons orange marmalade

2 tablespoons Cointreau

Method:

1. Heat oven to 325 °F (160 °C).

2. Whisk butter, 1/2 cup sugar and orange zest until smooth. Whisk in egg yolks, then flour, until smooth.

3. Whisk in orange juice, 2 tablespoons lemon juice, and milk.

4. In a separate bowl, beat egg whites until foamy. Gradually add remaining 1/4 cup sugar, until stiff and shiny

5. Fold whites into batter.

6. Spray eight ramekins with cooking spray. Set them in 2 large baking pans, half filled with water

7. Pour batter into each ramekin.

8. Bake 25 to 35 minutes, until golden.

9. Allow to cool to a warm temperature, and invert onto dessert plate.

10. Mix together marmalade, Cointreau and remaining 2 lemon juice. Spoon over cakes.

Fried Bananas with Chocolate Cointreau Sauce

Serves 6

Ingredients:

1/2 cup semisweet chocolate chips

1/3 cup whipping cream

1/2 teaspoon vanilla extract

1/2 cup Cointreau

1 tablespoon butter

6 bananas, peeled and halved lengthwise

1 cup toasted sliced almonds

Method:

1. Stir together chocolate chips, cream, and vanilla extract over a medium-low heat until chocolate has melted. Stir in Cointreau and set aside.

2. Melt butter in a pan over medium-high heat. Add bananas and cook until browned. Turn bananas and brown on the other side.

3. Place two banana halves onto each plate, pour chocolate Cointreau sauce over the top and sprinkle with toasted almonds.

Grand Marnier Soufflé

Serves 2

Ingredients:

1 tablespoon butter, melted

1 tablespoon white sugar

5 teaspoons butter

5 teaspoons all-purpose flour

1/4 cup cold milk

2 egg yolks

1 teaspoon orange zest, freshly grated

1 tablespoon Grand Marnier

1/8 teaspoon vanilla extract

2 egg whites

1/4 cup white sugar, divided

Method:

1. Preheat oven to 400 °F (200 °C).
2. Brush 2 ramekins with 1 tablespoon melted butter and sprinkle with 1 tablespoon sugar.
3. Place on a baking sheet lined with aluminum foil.
4. Melt 5 teaspoons butter in a saucepan and stir in flour until golden brown.
5. Slowly add milk, stirring continuously, until thickened.
6. Combine milk mixture, orange zest, and Grand Marnier in a bowl and mix well.
7. Add egg yolks and vanilla.
8. Whisk egg whites until soft peaks. Slowly add sugar, whisking constantly until thick and shiny.
10. Fold egg whites into egg yolk mixture.
11. Pour mixture evenly into ramekins.
12. Bake for 16 minutes.

Grand Marnier-Glazed Strawberry Pie

Serves 8

Ingredients:

1 (9 inch) refrigerated pie crust

1 cup fresh strawberries, hulled

3/4 cup water

3/4 cup white sugar

3 tablespoons cornstarch

3 tablespoons Grand Marnier

3 cups fresh strawberries, hulled

Method:

1. Preheat an oven to 400 °F (200 °C).

2. Bake pie crust 20 minutes or until golden brown.

3. Puree 1 cup of strawberries and place in a saucepan. Stir in water, sugar, and cornstarch and stir over medium heat until thickened.

4. Remove from heat and stir in Grand Marnier. Set aside.

5. Place remaining strawberries in pie crust and pour the glaze over the berries.

6. Refrigerate until glaze is set.

Cointreau Truffles

Serves 12

Ingredients:

1/4 cup butter, unsalted

3 tablespoons heavy cream

4oz (120g) semisweet chocolate, chopped

2 tablespoons Cointreau

1 teaspoon orange zest grated

4oz (120g) semisweet chocolate, chopped

1 tablespoon vegetable oil

Method:

1. Combine butter and cream in a saucepan and bring to a boil.
2. Remove from heat and stir in 4oz (120g) chocolate, Cointreau, and orange zest until smooth.
3. Refrigerate until firm.
4. Roll into balls and place on baking tray lined with wax paper and refrigerate again.
5. Melt remaining chocolate with oil, over a double boiler. Allow to cool slightly.
6. Coat truffles in melted chocolate. Replace onto baking tray and refrigerate until set.

Gingerbread Cointreau Cheesecake

Serves 12

Ingredients:

8oz (225g) gingernut cookies

1/2 cup butter, melted

1/4 cup Cointreau

Pinch of saffron threads

15oz (425g) cream cheese

1/2 cup honey

1 1/2 tablespoons orange zest, finely-grated

1 3/4 cups heavy cream

Method:

1. Blend cookies and butter in a blender until moist and crumbly.
2. Press into a 9 inch pan and refrigerate.
3. Heat Cointreau in a saucepan until it begins to steam and add saffron threads.
4. Remove from heat and set aside for 20 minutes.
5. Beat cream cheese and slowly beat in honey, orange zest and saffron mixture.
6. Continuing to beat, slowly add cream until thick.
7. Spoon the mixture over the base and chill overnight.

Cointreau Cream Strawberries

Serves 4

Ingredients:

1 pint fresh strawberries

8oz (225g) cream cheese, softened

1/2 cup confectioners' sugar

2 tablespoons Cointreau

Method:

1. Cut the tops off of the strawberries and stand upside down.
2. Make a cut 3/4 of the way down from the tip of the strawberry towards the bottom.
3. Beat together the cream cheese, sugar, and Cointreau until smooth.
4. Pipe mixture into each strawberry.

Raspberry and Cointreau White Chocolate Mousse

Serves 16

Ingredients:

10oz (280g) frozen raspberries, thawed

2 tablespoons white sugar

2 tablespoons Cointreau

1 3/4 cups heavy whipping cream

6oz (170g) white chocolate, chopped

1 drop red food coloring

Method:

1. Puree berries and strain mixture into a small bowl, discarding seeds.

2. Add sugar and Cointreau, and stir until sugar dissolves.

3. Heat 1/4 cup of the cream and white chocolate over a low heat, stirring constantly until chocolate melts. Allow to cool slightly.

4. Stir in 1 tablespoon of raspberry mixture, and food coloring.

5. Whip remaining cream until soft peaks form.

6. Fold into chocolate mixture.

7. Layer into parfait dishes, and serve with the remaining sauce.

Kahlua

Kahlua is the brand name of a rum-based Mexican coffee liqueur with herbs and vanilla. It is the most well-known of the coffee liqueurs, and the brand name has become synonymous with the generic name. Any coffee liqueur can be substituted in these recipes, or for a non-alcoholic substitution consider either coffee essence or a strong brewed espresso.

Chocolate Chip Cookie Kahlua Milkshakes

Serves 2

Ingredients:

2 cups coffee icecream

1 1/2 cups milk

1/2 cup Kahlua

2 large chocolate chip cookies + 1 more to crumble on top

6 ice cubes

Method:

Blend all ingredients until smooth. Pour into glasses and crumble cookie on top.

Tiramisu

Serves 12

Ingredients:

6 egg yolks

1 1/4 cups white sugar

1 1/4 cups mascarpone cheese

1 3/4 cups heavy whipping cream

12oz (340g) ladyfingers

1/3 cup Kahlua

1 teaspoon unsweetened cocoa powder (for garnish)

1oz (30g) square semisweet chocolate, grated (for garnish)

Method:

1. Combine egg yolks and sugar in the top of a double boiler, over boiling water. Stir over a low heat for about 10 minutes.

2. Remove from heat and whip yolks until thick and lighter in color.

3. Beat in mascarpone.

4. In a separate bowl, whip cream until stiff. Fold into yolk mixture. Set aside.

5. Line the bottom and sides of a bowl with half of the ladyfingers 6. Brush with Kahlua. Spoon half of the cream filling over the ladyfingers.

7. Repeat the last step with remaining ingredients.

8. Garnish with cocoa and grated chocolate.

9. Refrigerate overnight.

Tiramisu Cheesecake

Serves 8

Ingredients:

12oz (340g) ladyfingers

4 tablespoons butter, melted

4 tablespoons Kahlua

24oz (680g) cream cheese

8oz (225g) mascarpone cheese

1 cup white sugar

2 eggs

4 tablespoons all-purpose flour

1oz (30g) square semisweet chocolate, grated

Method:

1. Preheat oven to 350 °F (175 °C).
2. Process ladyfingers to fine crumbs.
3. Mix melted butter into the crumbs.
4. Add 2 tablespoons of Kahlua. Press into a 9-inch pan.
5. Mix together cream cheese, mascarpone, and sugar.
6. Add remaining Kahlua, eggs and flour, and mix until smooth.
7. Pour filling into crust.
8. Bake for 40 minutes, or until set.
9. Turn off the heat and leave cake in oven to cool for 20 minutes.
10. Refrigerate and sprinkle with grated chocolate before serving.

Vanilla Mocha Cheesecake

Serves 8

Ingredients:

Crust:

1 cup vanilla wafers, crushed

2 tablespoons butter, melted

1 tablespoon white sugar

1 tablespoon unsweetened cocoa powder

Topping:

1 cup sour cream

2 tablespoons white sugar

1 teaspoon Kahlua

1 teaspoon unsweetened cocoa powder

Filling:

1 tablespoon instant coffee powder

2 tablespoons Kahlua

4oz (120g) semisweet chocolate, grated

32oz (900g) cream cheese

1 cup white sugar

4 eggs

Method:

Crust:

Combine vanilla wafer crumbs, melted butter, sugar, and cocoa and press into a 9-inch pan.

Filling:

1. Preheat oven to 350 °F (175 °C).
2. Place chocolate in the top of a double boiler and stir until almost melted.
3. Remove from heat and continue stirring until completely melted. Set aside.
4. Combine cream cheese and sugar and mix well.
5. Dissolve coffee powder in Kahlua.
6. Add coffee mixture and chocolate to the cream cheese mixture and mix well.
7. Add the eggs one at a time, mixing just until incorporated.
8. Pour filling into the crust and bake for 1 hour.
10. Spread topping over and return to the oven for 5 minutes. Refrigerate overnight.

Topping:

Mix together sour cream, sugar, Kahlua and cocoa.

Mudslide Brownies

Serves 36

Ingredients:

2/3 cup butter

4oz (120g) bittersweet chocolate, chopped

3 eggs

1 1/2 cups white sugar

1/4 cup Kahlua

2 tablespoons Baileys Irish cream

2 tablespoons vodka

2 cups all-purpose flour

1/2 teaspoon baking powder

3/4 cup chopped walnuts

Method:

1. Preheat oven to 350 °F (175 °C).

2. Melt butter and chocolate in microwave in 30 second intervals, stirring in between. Set aside.

3. Beat eggs and sugar until light.

4. Fold in the chocolate mixture, Kahlua, Baileys and vodka.

5. Combine flour and baking powder and stir into the chocolate mixture.

6. Add walnuts and stir lightly until just incorporated.

7. Bake in a 9x13 inch pan for 25 minutes.

8. Cut into squares and glaze with Kahlua and confectioners' sugar.

Kahlua Caramel Cups

Serves 12

Ingredients:

8oz (225g) cream cheese

2 cups all-purpose flour

1 cup butter flavored shortening

14oz (400g) caramels

1 can evaporated milk

2 teaspoons Kahlua

1/2 cup butter

1/2 cup shortening

2/3 cup white sugar

1 can evaporated milk

2 teaspoons Kahlua

Ground pecans (to garnish)

Method:

1. Preheat oven to 350 °F (175 °C).

2. Beat together the cream cheese, flour, and butter flavored shortening. Press dough into mini cupcake tin.

3. Bake for 18 minutes.

4. Melt caramels in the top of a double boiler.

5. Remove from heat and stir in 1 can evaporated milk and 2 teaspoons of Kahlua. Set aside to thicken.

6. Combine butter, remaining shortening, remaining evaporated milk, white sugar and remaining Kahlua.

7. Beat for at least 8 minutes.

8. Using half the caramel mixture, half fill cups with caramel mixture. Wait 10 minutes and then top with the remaining mix.

9. Sprinkle with ground pecans.

Chocolate Cigars with Kahlua Mocha Cream

Serves 48

Ingredients:

Cigars:

2 cups confectioners' sugar, sifted

1 1/4 cups all-purpose flour, sifted

1/8 teaspoon salt

5/8 cup butter, melted and cooled

1 vanilla bean, split and scraped

6 egg whites

1 tablespoon heavy cream

1 1/2 ounces bittersweet chocolate, grated

Filling:

1/4 cup Kahlua

1 1/2 teaspoons instant coffee powder

2 1/2 cups heavy cream

1/4 cup confectioners' sugar

1 1/2oz (45g) bittersweet chocolate, grated

Method:

Cigars:

1. Preheat oven to 400 °F (200 °C).

2. Mix confectioners' sugar, flour and salt.

3. In a separate bowl, combine melted butter and vanilla scrapings.

4. Pour vanilla butter, egg whites and cream into dry ingredients and mix well.

5. Fold in grated chocolate. Refrigerate for 2 hours.

6. Line a baking tray with waxed paper and pour batter to make three 10cm circles.

7. Bake for 4 minutes.

8. Remove cigar quickly from tray, and while still warm and soft, roll into cigar shapes and leave to cool.

9. Repeat until remaining batter is used up.

Filling:

1. Mix together Kahlua and espresso powder until dissolved.

2. Beat in cream and confectioners' sugar

Mocha Log with Chocolate Ganache and Kahlua Syrup

Serves 16

Ingredients:

Kahlua Syrup:

1 cup granulated sugar

1 cup water

3 tablespoons Kahlua

Biscuit Roulade:

1/2 cup pastry flour or all-purpose flour, sifted

1 teaspoon baking powder, sifted

1/4 cup cocoa powder, sifted

4 egg yolks

1 cup sugar, divided

4 egg whites

Coffee Buttercream:

1 cup water

3 tablespoons ground coffee beans

1 cup fine granulated sugar

5 large egg whites

1 1/2 cups unsalted butter, cubed

2 teaspoons vanilla extract

Chocolate Ganache:

11 ounces dark chocolate

1 tablespoon butter

2 teaspoons honey

1 cup heavy whipping cream

Method:

Kahlua Syrup:

Heat sugar and water until the sugar is dissolved. Bring to a boil, then remove from heat and add Kahlua. Set aside to cool.

Biscuit Roulade:

1. Preheat oven to 375 °F (190 C).

2. Butter and flour a jelly-roll pan. Line bottom with buttered and floured waxed paper.

3. Combine flour, baking powder, and cocoa. Set aside.

4. Beat egg yolks until thick and lemon colored. Gradually add 1/2 5 cup of sugar, beating till the sugar is dissolved.

6. Beat egg whites until soft peaks form. Gradually add remaining sugar, beating till stiff peaks form.

7. Fold egg yolks into the egg whites.

8. Add dry ingredients and stir very gently until just incorporated.

9. Pour batter into jelly-roll pan and bake for 12 to 15 minutes, or until cooked.

10. Lay a kitchen towel on to a flat surface and dust with confectioners' sugar. Turn cake onto kitchen towel and remove waxed paper. Using the towel, roll the lengthwise, with the towel inside.

11. Lay with the seam underneath and leave to cool.

12. Unroll and brush with Kahlua syrup.

13. Spread evenly with buttercream.

14. Reroll and pour ganache over the top.

Coffee Buttercream:

1. Boil 1/2 cup water and add coffee grinds. Allow to steep for 5 minutes then strain. Set aside.

2. Mix remaining water and sugar over medium-high heat until boiling.

3. Beat egg whites until soft peaks form. Gradually add sugar water, stirring constantly, and continue to beat until stiff.

4. Add butter and beat on high until smooth and shiny.

5. Add vanilla extract and coffee concentrate. Set aside.

Chocolate Ganache:

1. Mix together chocolate, butter, and honey.

2. Heat the whipping cream over medium heat until boiling. Pour into the chocolate mixture and whisk until smooth.

3. Allow to cool to room temperature.

Mocha Choca Truffles

Serves 36

Ingredients:

12oz (340g) semi-sweet chocolate

2 egg yolks

1/3 cup sweetened condensed milk

1/3 cup Kahlua

1/3 cup butter

1 tablespoon unsweetened cocoa powder

Method:

1. Melt chocolate in the top of a double boiler.

2. Remove from heat and stir in egg yolks, sweetened condensed milk and Kahlua then to heat. Simmer until heated.

3. In a mixer bowl, combine chocolate mixture and butter and beat until fluffy.

4. Cover and refrigerate for 4 hours or more.

5. Roll mixture into balls.

6. Roll balls in cocoa powder until coated.

7. Refrigerate.

White Chocolate Mudslide Shots

Serves 24

Ingredients:

2 cups heavy whipping cream

2 packages instant white chocolate pudding mix

6fl oz (180ml) Baileys Irish cream

2fl oz (60ml) Kahlua

Method:

1. Beat cream until stiff peaks form.

2. Add pudding mix and beat until firm.

3. Stir in Baileys and Kahlua.

4. Spoon pudding mixture into mini cupcake tray. .

5. Freeze until set.

Amarula

Amarula is a South African cream liqueur made from the fruit of the African marula tree. This unique cream has a delicious, creamy fruit taste, with a slightly nutty aftertaste and is light brown in color. While it has the same creaminess as Irish cream, it is lighter in both texture and taste. There is really no substitute for this distinctive beverage, so if you do not want to use alcohol, it is best to choose another recipe.

Amarula Chocolate Fondue

Ingredients:

1/2 cup whipping cream

1/2 cup Amarula liqueur

2 cups semisweet chocolate chips

1 dash vanilla extract

Method:

1. Combine whipping cream and amarula liqueur in a fondue pot.

2. Stir over a medium-low heat until mixture boils.

3. Reduce to a low heat and stir in the chocolate chips until melted.

4. Stir in the vanilla.

Amaretto

Amaretto is an almond-flavored Italian liqueur. While some amaretto is made from almonds, others are made from apricot pits and do not contain almonds at all. The sweet, nutty beverage is perfect by itself as an after-dinner tipple, or added to coffee for a unique twist. Its nutty taste lends itself to many sweet dishes. For a non-alcoholic substitution, use almond essence.

Oreo Amaretto Layered Cream Pie

Serves 8

Ingredients:

3 cups heavy cream

1/4 cup amaretto

3 tablespoons sugar

2 teaspoons vanilla extract

2 packets Oreos

Method:

1. Whisk together heavy cream, almond liqueur, sugar and vanilla extract until it forms soft peaks.

2. Arrange a single layer of Oreos in a trifle dish.

3. Spread 1/2 cup cream mixture over the Oreos.

4. Repeat Oreo/cream alternation until complete.

5. Crumble one Oreo over the top layer of cream.

6. Cover and refrigerate overnight.

Amaretto Cannoli Tart

Serves 6

Ingredients:

Crust:

2 cups flour, sifted

1/2 cup + 1 tablespoon sugar

1/2 teaspoon salt

1 teaspoon cinnamon

1/3 cup butter

1 whole egg

1 tablespoon milk

Filling:

2 1/4 cups ricotta

1 whole egg

2 teaspoons sugar

2 teaspoons amaretto

1/2 cups chocolate chips or chunks

Method:

Crust:

1. Blend flour, sugar, salt, cinnamon and butter until crumbed.

2. Add egg and milk and pulse until a large ball is formed.

3. Mix in egg and milk and knead into a ball.

4. Roll dough and place in a greased deep dish pan.

5. Refrigerate while making filling.

Filling:

1. Preheat oven to 350 °F (175 °C)

2. Blend together ricotta, egg, sugar, and amaretto. Add chocolate chips.

3. Pour filling into crust.

4. Bake 25-35 minutes, or until done.

5. Refrigerate.

Amaretto Cheesecake

Serves 16

Ingredients:

32oz (900g) cream cheese, softened

1 cup unsalted butter, softened

1 1/2 cups sour cream

1/2 cup heavy whipping cream

1 3/4 cups white sugar

1/8 cup cornstarch

1fl oz (30ml) amaretto

1 teaspoon vanilla extract

5 eggs

1 egg yolk

Method:

1. Preheat oven to 375 °F (190 °C).

2. Beat cream cheese and butter until smooth. Mix in sugar, cornstarch, sour cream, whipping cream, amaretto and vanilla.

3. Stir in eggs and egg yolk one at a time, mixing each thoroughly before adding the next.

4. Pour batter into a well-greased 9-inch pan.

5. Place pan into a larger pan half filled with water.

6. Bake for 70 minutes.

7. Turn oven off, leave the door open, and allow to cool for one hour.

8. Refrigerate for 4 hours or more.

Vanilla Amaretto Pudding

Serves 12

Ingredients:

2 packages instant vanilla pudding mix

2 cups whole milk

1 can sweetened condensed milk

1 tablespoon lemon juice

1/2 cup amaretto

1 teaspoon vanilla extract

16oz (450g) frozen whipped topping, thawed

5 bananas, sliced

8oz (225g) vanilla wafer cookies

Method:

1. Mix together pudding mix, milk and condensed milk.

2. Add lemon juice, amaretto and vanilla.

3. Fold in whipped topping.

4. In a serving bowl, create layers of pudding mixture, bananas and cookies.

5. Refrigerate.

Chocolate Amaretto Sorbet

Serves 8

Ingredients:

1 cup sugar

3/4 cup unsweetened cocoa powder

1 1/2 cups water

2 tablespoons amaretto

Method:

1. In a medium bowl, whisk together sugar, cocoa, water, and amaretto until smooth.

2. Pour mixture into an ice cream freezer container, and follow the manufacturer's instructions to freeze.

Chocolate Amaretto Torte

Serves 12

Ingredients:

1/3 cup cake flour, sifted	1/2 cup white sugar
3 tablespoons unsweetened cocoa powder	5 teaspoons cornstarch
1/4 cup white sugar	1/4 teaspoon salt
6 egg whites	1/4 cup white sugar
1/2 teaspoon cream of tartar	1 cup milk
1/4 teaspoon salt	2 eggs
1 teaspoon vanilla extract	2 tablespoons amaretto

Method:

Torte:

1. Preheat oven to 375 °F (190 °C).

2. Sift together flour, cocoa, and 1/4 cup of white sugar.

3. Beat egg whites, cream of tartar and salt until soft peaks form.

4. Gradually add 1/2 cup sugar until stiff and shiny.

5. Add vanilla.

6. Slowly fold dry mixture into egg whites.

7. Pour filling into a loaf pan.

8. Bake for 25 minutes or until cooked. Allow to cool.

9. Cut into 3 layers and spread almond filling between the layers and dust top with sifted confectioners' sugar.

Filling:

1. Combine remaining white sugar, cornstarch and salt in a saucepan.

2. Beat eggs and milk together and add to sugar mixture.

3. Stir over medium heat, until thick and bubbling.

4. Remove from heat and stir in amaretto.

5. Cover and refrigerate.

Amaretto Icecream

Serves 12

Ingredients:

2 cups heavy whipping cream

1 cup half-and-half

3/4 cup white sugar

5 tablespoons amaretto

1 teaspoon vanilla extract

Method:

1. Mix together heavy cream, half-and-half, and sugar until sugar dissolves. Add amaretto and vanilla extract.

2. Either use your icecream maker as per manufacturer's instructions, or place in freezer, stirring vigorously every 30 minutes.

Baileys Irish Cream

Baileys Irish cream is a whiskey-based, cream liqueur. There are many different Irish creams on the market now, however Baileys was the first, created in 1974, and the brand name is now synonymous with the generic term. The smooth, creamy liqueur is able to be substituted for any Irish cream liqueur.

Baileys Crème Brûlée

Serves 6

Ingredients:

2 cups heavy cream

1/3 cup white sugar

6 egg yolks

1 teaspoon vanilla extract

3 tablespoons Baileys Irish cream

Superfine sugar, as needed

Method:

1. Preheat oven to 300 °F (150 °C).

2. Stir cream and sugar over medium heat until the sugar dissolves.

3. Whisk together egg yolks, vanilla, and Baileys Irish cream.

4. Gradually add hot cream, 1/3 at a time, whisking constantly. This may go through a curdled-looking stage, this is normal.

5. Pour mixture into 6 ramekins, and place into a larger pan half filled with water.

6. Bake 50 to 60 minutes, until set.

7. Refrigerate for 4 hours or more.

8. Sprinkle 1 teaspoon sugar onto each ramekin.

9. To serve: use a small hand torch to melt sugar until it caramelizes.

Baileys Chocolate Mousse

Serves 4

Ingredients:

4oz (120g) dark chocolate, chopped

3 eggs, separated

1 tablespoon Baileys Irish cream

1 cup whipped cream

Chocolate shavings (for garnish)

Method:

1. Stir dark chocolate in a double boiler until almost melted, then remove from heat and continue to stir until melted.
2. Stir in beaten egg yolks and Baileys Irish cream.
3. Fold in 1/2 of the whipped cream.
4. In a separate bowl, beat the egg whites until stiff and fold into chocolate mixture.
5. Pour mixture into dessert bowls and refrigerate.
6. To serve: garnish with chocolate shavings.

Baileys Macadamia Pie

Serves 8

Ingredients:

5 eggs

1 1/4 cups white sugar

1/2 tablespoon salt

3/4 cup butter

1 cup light corn syrup

3/4 cup Baileys Irish cream

1 1/3 cups semisweet chocolate chips

2 cups macadamia nuts

1 (9 inch) pie crust

Method:

1. Cream eggs, salt, sugar, and butter.
2. Add corn syrup and Baileys Irish cream.
3. Add chocolate chips and nuts.
4. Pour filling into pie shell.
5. Bake for 1 1/2 hours.

Frozen Baileys Custard

Serves 24

Ingredients:

2 cans evaporated milk

3 cups whole milk

2 cups Baileys Irish cream

1 can sweetened condensed milk

1 cup brown sugar

1/4 cup white sugar

5 eggs

1/2 teaspoon ground cinnamon

1 pinch ground nutmeg

Pinch of salt

1 vanilla bean

Method:

1. Beat all ingredients, except vanilla bean.

2. Slice vanilla bean and scrape seeds into the mixture. Add vanilla bean pod.

3. Transfer to a saucepan, and stir over a medium heat until thickened. Remove from heat and allow to cool.

4. Blend mixture in a blender until smooth.

5. Refrigerate 2 hours or more.

6. Either use your icecream maker as per manufacturer's instructions, or place in freezer, stirring vigorously every 30 minutes.

Baileys Peanut Butter Frozen Yoghurt

Serves 10

Ingredients:

3 cups non-fat Greek yoghurt

1 cup white sugar

3/4 cup peanut butter

1/2 cup Baileys Irish cream

1 teaspoon vanilla extract

Method:

Beat all ingredients well. Either use your icecream maker as per manufacturer's instructions, or place in freezer, stirring vigorously every 30 minutes.

Kirsch

Kirsch is a clear-colored cherry brandy originating in Germany. It is usually drunk cold and neat as an aperitif. For a non-alcoholic substitute, consider cherry essence, cherry concentrate, or cherry juice boiled until reduced to a syrup.

Cherry Clafouti

Serves 8

Ingredients:

1 1/2 pounds fresh sweet cherries, pitted

1 tablespoon unsalted butter

3 tablespoons all-purpose flour

1/2 teaspoon salt

1/4 cup white sugar

8 egg whites

1 cup skim milk

1 cup heavy cream

1 vanilla bean, split and crushed

3 tablespoons kirsch

1 tablespoon confectioners' sugar (for garnish)

Method:

1. Preheat the oven to 325 °F (165 °C).

2. Arrange cherries in a greased 9 inch pan, and set aside.

3. Whisk together flour, salt and sugar.

4. In a separate bowl, whisk together the egg whites, milk and cream. Add kirsch and vanilla bean.

5. Gradually add flour mixture, whisking until smooth.

6. Remove vanilla bean and pour mixture over the cherries.

7. Bake for 45 minutes.

8. To serve: Dust with confectioners' sugar.

Limoncello

Limoncello is a sweet lemon liqueur originating in Italy. It is usually drunk cold and neat after dinner as a digestivo. For a non-alcoholic substitute, consider lemon essence, lemon concentrate, or lemon juice boiled until reduced to a syrup.

Lemon Berry Savarin

Serves 8

Ingredients:

Savarin:

2 1/4 cups all-purpose flour, divided

1 envelope rapid rise yeast

1/4 cup sugar

1/2 teaspoon salt

1/2 cup milk

10 tablespoons butter, cubed

4 large eggs

1 tablespoon grated lemon zest

Syrup:

1 1/2 cups sugar

1 cup water

1/2 cup each lemon juice and limoncello

1 quart strawberries

1 pint raspberries

Method:

1. Preheat oven to 375 °F (190 °C).
2. Combine 3/4 cup flour, yeast, sugar and salt.
3. Heat milk and butter until very warm.
4. Gradually add milk mixture to flour mixture; stirring constantly.
5. Beat eggs, 1 cup flour and lemon zest for 2 minutes. Stir in remaining 1/2 cup flour until blended.
6. Press dough into a greased and floured ring pan.
7. Cover and set aside to rise until doubled in size.
8. Bring sugar and water to a boil then reduce heat and simmer until syrupy.
9. Remove from heat and stir in lemon juice and limoncello.
10. Bake for 25 minutes or until done.
11. Prick holes into the surface and brush with half of the syrup.
12. Spoon or brush remaining syrup over cake.
13. Place berries in center of the ring.

Rum

Rum adds flavor and warmth to robust dishes, such as chocolate. For a more robust taste, choose a darker rum; for a more subtle taste, choose a lighter rum. Rum essence can be substituted for smaller amounts of rum, but for larger amounts, you are better to choose another dish.

Frozen Chocolate Rum Nougat

Serves 8

Ingredients:

6oz (170g) almond nougat

4 eggs whites

6 egg yolks

6 tablespoons sugar

2 cups heavy whipping cream

1/2 cup bittersweet chocolate, chopped

1 tablespoon dark rum

Pinch of salt

Method:

1. Cut nougat into small pieces then process in a food processor until crumbed.

2. Whip together egg yolks and sugar.

3. In a separate bowl, whip cream until peaks form.

4. Combine whipped cream, chocolate, rum, 1 1/4 cup of the ground nougat and egg yolks, mixing well.

5. In a separate bowl, whip egg whites together with a pinch of salt until stiff peaks form. Fold gently into nougat mixture.

6. Sprinkle remaining crumbed nougat on the inside of a bowl then pour in the nougat mixture.

7. Cover and freeze.

Rum Cream Pie

Serves 8

Ingredients:

1 cup graham cracker crumbs

2 tablespoons white sugar

3 tablespoons melted butter

1/4 cup cold water

1 cup heavy cream

1/4 cup rum

3 egg yolks

1/2 cup white sugar

1/2 package unflavored gelatin

1/8 cup semisweet chocolate, grated (for garnish)

Method:

1. Preheat oven to 325 °F (165 °C).

2. Combine graham cracker crumbs, 2 tablespoons sugar and butter. Press firmly into a 9 inch pan.

3. Bake for 10 minutes. Set aside to cool.

4. Sprinkle gelatin over the cold water and set aside to soften.

5. Whisk egg yolks and sugar in a heatproof bowl until thick and lighter in color. Stir over a pot of simmering water for 5 minutes.

6. Remove from heat and stir in gelatin until dissolved. Set aside to cool.

7. In a separate bowl whip the cream to peaks then mix in rum.

8. Fold whipped cream into egg mixture.

9. Pour mixture into pie base and garnish with grated chocolate.

10. Chill for 6 hours.

Eggnog Cheesecake

Serves 16

Ingredients:

1 cup graham cracker crumbs

2 tablespoons white sugar

3 tablespoons melted butter

1 cup white sugar

3 tablespoons all-purpose flour

3/4 cup eggnog

2 eggs

2 tablespoons rum

1 pinch ground nutmeg

24oz (680g) packages cream cheese, softened

Method:

1. Preheat oven to 325 °F (165 °C).

2. Combine graham cracker crumbs, 2 tablespoons sugar and butter. Press firmly into a 9 inch pan.

3. Bake for 10 minutes. Set aside to cool.

4. Preheat oven to 425 °F (220 °C).

5. Combine cream cheese, 1 cup sugar, flour and eggnog and beat well.

6. Add eggs, rum and nutmeg.

7. Pour mixture into cheesecake base and bake for 10 minutes.

8. Reduce heat to 250 °F (120 °C) and bake for 45 minutes.

Rum Balls

Serves 24

Ingredients:

1 cup semisweet chocolate chips

1/2 cup white sugar

3 tablespoons corn syrup

1/2 cup rum

2 1/2 cups crushed vanilla wafers

1 cup chopped walnuts (optional)

1/3 cup confectioners' sugar

Method:

1. Heat chocolate chips in the microwave for 1 minute. Sir then heat for 20 second intervals, stirring in between each, until melted.

2. Stir in remaining Ingredients and mix well. Refrigerate until firm.

4. Once firm, roll the mixture into bite-size balls. Roll balls in a mixture of ground nuts and confectioner's sugar.

5. You can eat immediately or, for best results, store for a week for flavors to infuse and enhance.

Bananas Foster

Serves 4

Ingredients:

1/4 cup butter

2/3 cup dark brown sugar

3 1/2 tablespoons rum

1 1/2 teaspoons vanilla extract

1/2 teaspoon ground cinnamon

3 bananas, sliced lengthwise and crosswise

1/4 cup walnuts, coarsely chopped

16oz (450g) vanilla ice cream

Method:

1. Melt butter over a medium heat.

2. Stir in sugar, rum, vanilla and cinnamon.

3. When mixture bubbles, add bananas and walnuts.

4. Cook 1-2 minutes or until bananas are hot.

5. Serve over vanilla ice cream.

Eggnog Cream Pie

Serves 8

Ingredients:

1 cup graham cracker crumbs

2 tablespoons white sugar

3 tablespoons melted butter

1 (4.6 oz, 130g) package non-instant vanilla pudding mix

1/4 teaspoon ground nutmeg

1 1/2 cups eggnog

2 teaspoons rum

2 cups heavy cream

1 pinch ground nutmeg, (for garnish)

Method:

1. Preheat oven to 325 °F (165 °C).

2. Combine graham cracker crumbs, 2 tablespoons sugar and butter. Press firmly into a 9 inch pan.

3. Bake for 10 minutes. Set aside to cool.

4. In a medium saucepan, combine pudding mix, nutmeg, and eggnog.

5. Stir over medium heat, until thick and bubbly.

6. Remove from heat, and stir in rum.

7. Cover and refrigerate until cool.

8. Whip the cream into peaks and fold into eggnog mixture.

9. Pour mixture into pie base and chill for four hours or longer.

Flambéed Vanilla Poached Pears with Apricot Sauce

Serves 6

Ingredients:

1 1/2 cups water

3/4 cup white sugar

1/2 teaspoon vanilla extract

6 Bosc pears, peeled, halved and cored

1 cup apricot preserves

2 tablespoons cornstarch

2 tablespoons water

1/2 cup rum

Method:

1. In a saucepan, boil 1 1/2 cups water, sugar, and vanilla extract to a boil.

2. Over a medium heat, simmer 3 pear halves at a time until tender.

3. Once all the pears are cooked, increase the heat slightly, and boil the syrup until reduced to 1 cup.

4. Stir in apricot preserves and once boiling, reduce to a simmer.

5. Dissolve cornstarch in 2 tablespoons of water and stir into syrup, stirring until thickened (about 30 seconds).

6. Pour sauce over pears, and sprinkle with the rum.

7. Carefully ignite the rum and let the alcohol burn out before serving.

Flan de Mango

Serves 12

Ingredients:

1 cup white sugar

1 tablespoon lemon juice

2 cups pureed mango

1 can sweetened condensed milk

2 tablespoons cornstarch

1 tablespoon rum (optional)

1 cup evaporated milk

6 eggs, beaten

1 pinch salt

Method:

1. Preheat oven to 350 °F (175 °C).

2. Fill a large, shallow baking pan with water 1 to 2 inches deep.

3. Mix together sugar and lemon juice in a saucepan over medium heat, stirring constantly until caramelized.

4. Remove from heat and stir in remaining Ingredients.

5. Pour into an 8x13 baking pan and place the entire pan into the pan with the water.

6. Bake 45 minutes, or until firm.

7. Set aside to cool before turning out.

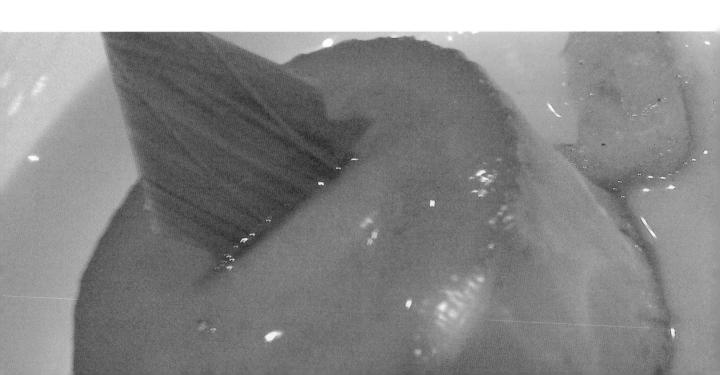

Kaiserschmarrn

Serves 4

Ingredients:

1/4 cup raisins	Salt
1/4 cup rum	1 cup all-purpose flour
1 cup whole milk	2 tablespoons butter
5 eggs	1 tablespoon butter, melted
1/4 cup white sugar	1/4 cup confectioners' sugar
1/2 teaspoon vanilla extract	

Method:

1. Soak raisins in rum for 30 minutes. Drain.

2. In a mixing bowl, beat together milk, eggs, white sugar, vanilla, and salt.

3. Slowly add flour.

4. Stir in the drained raisins.

5. Cook as you would with pancakes, then, while still in the pan, tear into smaller pieces.

6. Drizzle in the melted butter and sprinkle with confectioners' sugar. Toss the pieces over a medium high heat until the sugar has caramelized.

Mocha Panna Cotta with Chocolate-Rum Sauce

Serves 8

Ingredients:

2 teaspoons unflavored gelatin

1/4 cup dark rum

1 1/4 cups whipping cream

1/2 cup dark brown sugar

1 tablespoon instant espresso powder

1 cup coconut milk

1 teaspoon vanilla extract

1 cup sour cream

3/4 cup whipping cream

2 tablespoons dark colored corn syrup

8 ounces bittersweet chocolate, chopped

1 tablespoon dark rum

Sprigs fresh mint (for garnish)

Method:

1. Sprinkle gelatin over 1/4 cup of dark rum until soft.

2. Combine 1 1/4 cups whipping cream, brown sugar, and espresso powder in a saucepan over medium-high heat and bring to a simmer, stirring until sugar dissolved.

3. Remove from heat and stir in gelatin and rum mixture until dissolved.

4. Add coconut milk, vanilla extract, and sour cream and whisk until smooth.

5. Divide mixture into 8 bowls or molds.

6. Cover and refrigerate 4 hours or more.

7. Combine remaining whipping cream and corn syrup in a saucepan and bring to a simmer.

8. Remove from heat, and stir in the chocolate until melted. Stir in 1 tablespoon of rum and set aside to cool.

9. When ready to serve, place each cup into a shallow bowl of hot water for 10 seconds to loosen, then turn the mold over a serving plate.

10. Spoon chocolate rum sauce over each panna cotta and garnish with mint.

Vegan Chocolate Rum Cheesecake

Serves 12

Ingredients:

1 cup ground almonds

1 cup whole wheat flour

2/3 cup vegan margarine

12oz (340g) firm tofu

1 1/2 cups Demerara sugar

7 tablespoons unsweetened cocoa powder

1/4 cup sunflower seed oil

1/2 cup soy milk

1/4 cup dark rum

1 1/2 teaspoons vanilla extract

Method:

1. Preheat oven to 325 °F (165 °C)

2. Combine ground almonds and whole wheat flour. Cut in margarine until the texture of dough.

3. Press dough into a 9 inch pan.

4. Crumble the tofu in a food processor. Add sugar, cocoa, oil, soy milk, rum and vanilla and process until smooth.

5. Pour filling into crust.

6. Bake for 75 minutes, or until set.

Rum-Infused Banana Fudge Pie

Serves 8

Ingredients:

1 package instant vanilla pudding mix

1 1/4 cups cold milk

12oz (340g) frozen whipped topping, thawed, divided

2 bananas, sliced lengthways

1 (9 inch) prepared chocolate crumb crust

12oz (340g) hot fudge topping

2 tablespoons dark rum

1 can pineapple chunks, drained

12 maraschino cherries with stems, drained (for garnish)

3 tablespoons walnut pieces (for garnish)

Method:

1. Whisk together pudding mix and milk.

2. Fold in 2 cups of the whipped topping, and sliced banana. Set aside 1/2 of the banana cream mixture, and pour the remaining mixture into pie base.

3. Stir together hot fudge sauce and rum. Reserve 3 tablespoons for garnishing. Layer 1/2 the fudge sauce over banana cream mixture in pie base.

4. Repeat layering with remaining banana cream mixture and fudge sauce.

5. Refrigerate until firm.

6. Layer pineapple over pie. Top with remaining whipped topping, and refrigerate for 30 minutes.

7. Heat the 3 tablespoons of reserved fudge sauce 10 seconds and drizzle over top of pie.

8. Garnish with maraschino cherries and chopped walnuts.

Golden Rum Wonton Cannoli

Serves 20

Ingredients:

Cannoli:
20 wonton sheets

4 tablespoon butter, melted

Filling:
16oz (450g)mascarpone cheese

6 tablespoons butter, browned

2 tablespoons gold rum

4 cups confectioners' sugar

6oz (170g) chocolate, melted

4oz (120g) almonds, crushed

Method:

Cannoli:

1. Preheat oven to 375 °F (190 °C).

2. Use a round cookie cutter to cut out circles from each wonton sheet.

3. Brush melted butter over wonton circles.

4. Wrap wonton around cannoli form and bake at 375 °F (190 °C) for about 5 minutes or until golden brown.

5. Remove cannoli form and allow to cool.

6. Dip ends of cannoli cookie into melted chocolate then into crushed almonds. Allow chocolate to set.

7. Pipe filling into cookies and drizzle with remaining chocolate and dust with confectioners' sugar.

Filling:

1. Brown butter. Set aside to cool

2. Stir rum into cooled butter.

3. Cream mascarpone and confectioners' sugar.

4. Beat in butter mixture.

Pina Colada Cheesecake

Serves 10

Ingredients:

1 1/4 cups vanilla wafer crumbs

1 cup flaked coconut, toasted

1/2 cup butter, melted

6oz (170g) pineapple juice

1 (.25oz, 7g) package unflavored gelatin

24oz (680g) cream cheese, softened

3/4 cup sugar

1/4 cup dark Jamaican rum*

3/4 teaspoon coconut extract

2 cups frozen whipped topping, thawed

20oz (560g) crushed pineapple

1 tablespoon cornstarch

2 tablespoons sugar

Toasted flaked coconut (for garnish)

Method:

1. Combine crumbs, coconut and butter. Press mixture on bottom 9-inch pan. Set aside in refrigerator.

2. Pour juice into saucepan. Sprinkle gelatin over juice and leave to soften.

3. Stir over medium heat until gelatin dissolves. Set aside.

4. Beat together cream cheese and 3/4 cup sugar. Beat in gelatin mixture, rum and coconut extract.

5. Fold in whipped topping. Pour filling into cheesecake base.

6. Refrigerate at least 6 hours.

7. Combine undrained pineapple, cornstarch and 2 tablespoons sugar in a saucepan and stir until mixture boils and slightly thickens. Refrigerate.

8. To serve, spoon pineapple mixture over top of cheesecake.

9. Garnish with additional toasted coconut, if desired.

Cruschickies

Serves 48

Ingredients:

3 eggs

3 tablespoons white sugar

1/2 cup sour cream

1 teaspoon vanilla extract

2 tablespoons rum or brandy

1/4 teaspoon salt

3 1/3 cups all-purpose flour

4 cups vegetable oil

1/2 cup confectioners' sugar

Method:

1. Beat eggs and sugar. Mix in sour cream, vanilla and rum or brandy.

2. Slowly add sifted flour and salt, mixing to keep smooth, until a dough consistency. Knead dough.

3. Cut off a small portion of dough and roll out as thin as possible (almost paper thin).

4. To prepare the cruschickies, cut the dough into 2-inch wide strips, and cut these diagonally every 4 inches. In the middle of each strip, cut a one inch slit. Pull one corner through the slit.

5. Heat oil to 350 °F (175 °C).

6. Carefully lower a few cruschickies into the oil. When the lower side is brown, flip them and brown the other side. Then remove from oil and drain on a paper towel. Dust with confectioners' sugar.

Rum-Infused Mousse Cheesecake

Serves 8

Ingredients:

4oz (120g) semisweet chocolate, chopped

1 1/2 teaspoons unflavored gelatin

4 tablespoons cold water

8oz (225g) cream cheese

1 cup white sugar

2 tablespoons rum

2 egg yolks

6fl oz (180ml) heavy cream, whipped

2 egg whites

1 prepared chocolate cookie crumb crust

Method:

1. Sprinkle gelatin over water and allow to soften.

2. In the top of a double boiler, heat chocolate, stirring constantly until melted.

3. Place the bowl of gelatin over double boiler and stir until gelatin dissolves.

4. Cream the cream cheese and sugar until light and fluffy. Add rum, egg yolks, dissolved gelatin and melted chocolate.

5. Fold in whipped cream.

6. Whisk egg whites until stiff. Fold into chocolate mixture.

7. Pour filling into pie base.

8. Chill 4 hours or more.

Brandy

Brandy is a spirit made by the distillation of wine. It is typically imbibed as an after-dinner drink. Its high alcohol content makes it ideal for flambé, and is the traditional addition to crepe suzette and Christmas pudding. It may be substituted with brandy essence.

White Chocolate Cheesecake with White Chocolate Brandy Sauce

Serves 12

Ingredients:

White Chocolate Cheesecake:

4oz (120g) white chocolate

24oz (680g) cream cheese

3/4 cup white sugar

1/4 cup all-purpose flour

3 eggs

1/2 cup heavy cream

1/2 teaspoon vanilla extract

White Chocolate Brandy Sauce:

2 cups white chocolate, finely chopped

1 cup heavy cream

2fl oz (60ml) brandy

Method:

White Chocolate Cheesecake:

1. Preheat oven to 300 °F (150 °C).

2. Cream the cream cheese, sugar, and flour until light and fluffy.

3. Beat in eggs one at a time, mixing well after each addition.

4. Melt 4oz white chocolate and, with mixer on low speed, mix into cream cheese mixture. Slowly add in the vanilla and 1/2 cup of heavy cream. Pour filling into a greased pan.

5. Fill a larger pan 1 to 2 inches deep with water. Place cheesecake pan into this pan and bake for 50 to 60 minutes, or until center of the cheesecake is just firm.

6. Refrigerate.

White Chocolate Brandy Sauce:

1. Heat 1 cup heavy cream over a medium-high heat until it boils, then pour over chopped white chocolate. Stir until melted.

2. Add brandy. Pour over chilled cheesecake.

Gingerbread Cake with Grand Marnier Cream and Sweet Brandy Sauce

Serves 24

Ingredients:

Cake:

Cooking spray

7.5fl oz (220ml) vegetable oil

8oz (220g) white sugar

7.5 fl oz (220ml) molasses

2 large eggs

1 tablespoon freshly grated ginger

24oz (680g) plain flour

2 teaspoons ground cinnamon

1 teaspoon salt

1/4 teaspoon ground cloves

7.5fl oz (225ml) water

1 tablespoon bicarbonate of soda

Grand Marnier Cream:

15fl oz (450ml) double cream

1 teaspoon Grand Marnier

1 tablespoon confectioners' sugar

Pinch of cream of tartar

Brandy Sauce:

.5oz (15g) butter

2 tablespoons brandy

16oz (450g) confectioners' sugar

Method:

Cake:

1. Preheat oven to 300 °F (150 °C).

2. Whisk together the oil, sugar and molasses.

3. Whisk in eggs.

4. Stir in the ginger

5. In a separate bowl, whisk together the flour, cinnamon, salt and cloves.

6. Whisk in molasses mixture.

7. Bring water to a boil. Remove from the heat and stir in bicarbonate of soda.

8. Whisk water into mixture.

9. Pour mixture into 24 cupcake liners.

10. Bake 25 minutes or until done.

11. To serve: Add a dollop of Grand Marnier cream and drizzle with Brandy Sauce.

Cream:

Beat the whipping cream and Grand Marnier. Gradually add sugar and cream of tartar. Beat until stiff peaks form.

Brandy Sauce:

Melt butter and add brandy and confectioners' sugar.

Caramel Apple Brandy Cheesecake

Serves 8

Ingredients:

Cheesecake:

8 digestive biscuits

1 cup walnuts, lightly toasted

2 tablespoons light brown sugar

2.5oz (70g) unsalted butter, melted

1/2 cup plus 2 tablespoons caster sugar, divided

1 tablespoon orange zest

24oz (680g) packages cream cheese

1/2 cup plus 2 tablespoons packed light muscovado sugar

4 large eggs

Seeds from 1 large vanilla pod

1 teaspoon pure vanilla essence

1/2 teaspoon salt

4oz (120ml) double cream

16oz (480ml) apple juice

1/4 cup caster sugar

1 vanilla pod, seedless

.5oz (15g) cold butter

3 Granny Smith apples, peeled, seeded, thinly sliced

3 Fuji apples, peeled, seeded, thinly sliced

2fl oz (60ml) apple brandy

Caramel Sauce:

1 1/2 cups caster sugar

2fl oz (60ml) water

6oz (175ml) double cream

Pinch salt

3fl oz (45ml) apple brandy

1/2 teaspoon vanilla essence

Apples:

Method:

Cheesecake:

1. Preheat the oven to 355 °F (180 °C)

2. Blend digestive biscuits, 2oz (60g) of the walnuts and brown sugar until fine crumbs. Add butter and blend until the mixture comes together.

3. Press mixture evenly into the bottom of a greased 9 inch pan.

4. Bake 8 minutes and allow to cool.

5. Blend 1.7oz (50g) of the caster sugar and orange zest.

6. Beat cream cheese until light and fluffy.

7. Add the sugar mixture, remaining caster sugar and muscovado sugar and cream.

8. Add the eggs one at a time and mix until just combined. Add the vanilla seeds, vanilla essence, salt

and double cream.

9. Pour filling into the base. Place pan into a larger pan half filled with water.

10. Bake 55 minutes, then turn off oven and open oven door, and leave in oven to cool for 1 hour.

11. Refrigerate for 4 hours or more.

12. To serve: Top with apples, drizzle with caramel sauce and sprinkle walnuts to garnish.

Apples:

1. Boil apple juice, sugar and vanilla pod reduced to 120ml.

2. Add butter and stir until melted.

3. Add the apples, stirring occasionally, until tender.

4. Add the apple brandy and boil until reduced by half.

Sauce:

1. Boil caster sugar and water over high heat, occasionally gently swirling saucepan until amber in color (10-12 minutes).

2. While the caramel is cooking, bring double cream to a simmer.

3. When the caramel has reached the desired color, gradually whisk in the double cream and salt.

4. Remove from the heat and stir in the apple brandy and vanilla essence.

Brandied Walnut Pears

Serves 6

Ingredients:

1/3 cup brown sugar

1/3 cup water

1 tablespoon fresh lemon juice

3 large pears, peeled, halved, cored

1/3 cup walnuts, finely chopped

2 tablespoons brown sugar

1 1/2 tablespoons brandy

1 tablespoon plain yoghurt

1 cup whipping cream

1 tablespoon white sugar

2 teaspoons brandy

Method:

1. Preheat oven to 325 °F (165 °C).

2. Mix 1/3 cup brown sugar with water and lemon juice until dissolved.

3. Place pear halves, in a baking dish, and baste with the sauce brown sugar syrup.

4. Cover with foil and bake for 20 minutes until tender.

5. Mix walnuts together with remaining brown sugar, 1 1/2 tablespoons brandy, and yoghurt. Set aside.

6. Whip cream until stiff. Add white sugar and remaining 2 teaspoons of brandy.

7. Fill pear half with walnut mixture. Top with whipped cream. Serve warm.

Tequila

Tequila is a spirit made by distilling the fermented juice from the blue agave plant. Tequila is the national drink of Mexico and is widely recognized as a symbol of their culture and environment. In baking it pairs perfectly with lime. There are no non-alcoholic substitutions for tequila in baking, so simply skip smaller amounts, or for larger amounts, choose another dish.

Margarita Balls

Serves 48

Ingredients:

12oz (340g) vanilla wafers

2 cups small pretzel twists

6oz (170g) cream cheese

16oz (450g) confectioners' sugar

3/4 cup frozen margarita mix, thawed

2 tablespoons tequila

2 tablespoons Grand Marnier

1 tablespoon lime zest, grated

2/3 cup white sugar

4 drops green food coloring

Method:

1. Process vanilla wafers and pretzels to fine crumbs.

2. Combine crumbs with confectioners' sugar.

3. In a separate bowl, mix cream cheese, margarita mix, tequila and Grand Marnier. Stir into the crumb mixture.

4. Wrap and refrigerate for 2 hours or more.

5. In a small bowl combine sugar, food coloring and lime zest.

6. Roll dough into walnut sized balls.

7. Roll the balls in the green sugar.

Tequila Chilli Chocolate Fondue

Serves 2

Ingredients:

7oz (200g) dark chocolate

Pinch of dried chilli flakes

Pinch of ground cinnamon

Pinch of ground cayenne pepper

2.5fl oz (75ml) double cream

2 tablespoons tequila

Fresh mixed berries

Marshmallows

Method:

1. Place chocolate, chilli, cinnamon and cayenne in the top of a double boiler and stir until chocolate is melted a double boiler.

2. In a separate saucepan, warm cream, add the tequila, then add to the melted chocolate.

3. Dip fruit and marshmallows into the chocolate immediately.

Raspberry Tequila Nieve

Serves 4

Ingredients:

7oz (200g) caster sugar

17oz (500g) raspberries

Juice of 1/2 lime

3 tablespoons tequila

5fl oz (150ml) water

Method:

1. Boil 3/4 of the sugar with water for 3 minutes. Set aside.

2. Puree and strain raspberries and remaining sugar.

3. Combine sugar syrup and puree, and add lime juice and 1 tablespoon of the tequila.

4. Freeze for 2 hours.

5. Either use your icecream maker as per manufacturer's instructions, or place in freezer, stirring vigorously every hour.

6. To serve: pour a little tequila over the nieve.

Frozen Margarita Pie

Serves 8

Ingredients:

Crust:

1 cup pretzels, finely crushed

1/4 cup white sugar

1/3 cup butter, melted

Filling:

1 (14 ounce) can sweetened condensed milk

1/3 cup frozen limeade concentrate, thawed

2 tablespoons tequila

1 tablespoon Cointreau

3 drops green food coloring

1 cup heavy whipping cream

1 lime, sliced (for garnish)

Method:

Crust:

1. Preheat oven to 375 °F (190 °C).

2. Mix together pretzels, sugar and butter. Press into 9 inch pan.

3. Bake 5 minutes.

Filling:

1. Mix condensed milk, limeade concentrate, tequila, Cointreau, and green food coloring in a large bowl.

2. Beat cream until soft peaks form.

3. Fold whipped cream into condensed milk mixture.

4. Pour filling into base.

5. Cover and freeze until firm, about 4 hours.

6. Garnish with lime slices.

Margarita Cheesecakes Snacks

Serves 75

Ingredients:

1 can sweetened condensed milk

8oz (225g) cream cheese, softened

6oz (170g) frozen limeade concentrate

1/4 cup tequila

2 tablespoons triple sec

75 scoop-style tortilla chips

1 cup heavy whipping cream

2 teaspoons lime juice

2 tablespoons white sugar

Method:

1. Beat together condensed milk and cream cheese until smooth.

2. Add limeade, tequila, and triple sec; and beat until 5 to 8 minutes.

3. Spoon 1 tablespoon cheesecake mixture into each tortilla chip.

4. Refrigerate until set.

5. Beat cream and lime juice together smooth and thickened.

6. Gradually add sugar until soft peaks form.

7. Top each cheesecake with 1 teaspoon lime-flavored whipped cream.

Whiskey

Whiskey (also spelled "whisky") is a spirit made from distilled fermented grain aged in wooden barrels. The practice of distilling is so old, there is no discernable time that can be pointed to as the origin of whiskey. In baking, whiskey brings out the warmth in dishes, and enhances the flavor of more robust dishes. There are no non-alcoholic substitutions for tequila in baking, so simply skip smaller amounts, or for larger amounts, choose another dish.

Bourbon Praline Doughnuts

Serves 8

Ingredients:

Doughnuts:

3 cups plain flour

1 cup sugar

2 teaspoons baking powder

1 teaspoon bicarbonate of soda

1 teaspoon fine salt

2 tablespoons vegetable fat

6fl oz (180ml) buttermilk

1 large egg

1 large egg yolk

1 tablespoon vanilla essence

Vegetable oil

Bourbon praline, recipe follows

1/2 cup pecans, toasted, coarsely chopped (for garnish)

Whiskey Praline:

1 1/2 cups sugar

4fl oz (120ml) water

1/2 teaspoon vanilla extract

4fl oz (120ml) double cream

.5oz (14g) unsalted butter

1/4 teaspoon salt

1fl oz (30ml) bourbon whiskey

Method:

Doughnuts:

1. Mix together 300g of the flour, sugar, baking powder, bicarbonate of soda and salt.

2. Mix in vegetable fat.

3. In a separate bowl, whisk together the buttermilk, egg, egg yolk and vanilla.

4. Add buttermilk mixture to flour mixture and beat until smooth. Beat in remaining flour.

5. Cover and refrigerate for 1 hour or more.

6. Roll out dough to 1cm thick. Cut with a round cookie cutter. Using a smaller round cookie cutter, cut a hole from the centre of each round. The remaining dough can be rerolled and cut until used up.

7. Heat a deep pan of oil. Add the doughnuts, a few at a time, and fry until golden on both sides. Drain on paper towels and allow to cool.

8. Dip one side of the doughnuts into the bourbon-praline mixture and sprinkle nuts to garnish.

Whiskey Praline:

1. Heat sugar, water, vanilla pod and seeds over high heat and until a dark amber color.

2. Remove from the heat and gradually whisk in cream, butter and salt.

3. Return to heat and whisk until smooth.

4. Remove from heat and whisk in bourbon. Strain. Allow to cool and thicken.

Vanilla Bourbon Ciabatta Pudding

Serves 12

Ingredients:

Pudding:

1 1/2 pounds ciabatta, cubed

4 cups milk

1 1/2 sticks (170g) unsalted butter

1 cup packed light brown sugar

1/2 cup granulated sugar

3 tablespoons vanilla extract

5 large eggs, lightly beaten

1 cup golden raisins

Glaze:

4 tablespoons unsalted butter

2 tablespoons bourbon

1 cup confectioners' sugar

1/2 cup heavy cream

Method:

Pudding:

1. Preheat the oven to 350 °F (175 °C).

2. Pour half-and-half over bread and allow to soak.

3. Melt butter over medium heat. Remove from the heat, and stir in brown sugar, granulated sugar, and vanilla.

4. Whisk eggs, then stir in butter-sugar mixture.

5. Pour the custard mixture over bread, and stir to coat.

6. Pour mixture into a greased baking dish making sure bread is completely covered by mixture.

7. Sprinkle raisins over the top.

8. Cover the baking dish with aluminum foil and bake for 55 minutes.

9. Remove foil and bake for an additional 10 to 15 minutes, until golden brown.

10. To serve: pour glaze over pudding and let sit for 15 minutes.

Glaze:

1. Melt butter over medium heat.

2. Remove from heat and stir in bourbon and confectioners' sugar.

3. Mix in cream.

Bourbon Pecan Pie

Serves 8

Ingredients:

1/2 cup white sugar

1/2 cup brown sugar

3 tablespoons butter, melted

1/2 cup light corn syrup

3 eggs, beaten

2 tablespoons bourbon

2 cups pecan halves

1 (9 inch) unbaked deep-dish pie crust

Method:

1. Preheat the oven to 375 °F (190 °C)

2. Mix together white sugar, brown sugar, and butter.

3. Add corn syrup, eggs, and bourbon; fold in the pecans.

4. Pour mixture into the base.

5. Bake for 10 minutes; reduce heat to 350 °F (175 °C) and bake another 25 minutes.

Serves 8

Ingredients:

Cinnamon Crunch:

1/2 cup all-purpose flour

1/2 cup quick-cooking rolled oats

1/2 cup light muscovado sugar

1 teaspoon ground cinnamon

7 tablespoons unsalted butter, cubed

Crust:

2 cups graham cracker crumbs

8 tablespoons (1 stick) unsalted butter, melted

1/8 teaspoon ground cinnamon

1 large egg, lightly beaten

Bourbon-Maple Whipped Cream

1 1/4 cups heavy cream, very cold

2 teaspoons vanilla extract

2 tablespoons maple syrup

2 tablespoons bourbon

Filling:

3 large eggs

3 large egg yolks

3/4 cup dark muscovado sugar

1/4 cup granulated sugar

2 tablespoons molasses

1 1/2 cups pumpkin puree

1 1/4 teaspoons ground cinnamon

1 teaspoon ground ginger

1/2 teaspoon ground nutmeg

1/4 teaspoon ground cloves

1/2 teaspoon fine salt

1 cup heavy cream

1/2 cup whole milk

2 teaspoons vanilla extract

3 tablespoons unsalted butter, melted

Method:

Cinnamon Crunch:

1. Preheat oven to 350 °F (175 °C).

2. Blend flour, oats, muscovado sugar, and cinnamon in a food processor. Add the butter and blend until combined.

3. Press mixture onto a wax paper-lined baking sheet.

4. Bake 15 minutes or until golden.

5. Once cool, chop into small pieces.

Crust:

1. Mix together graham cracker crumbs, butter, and cinnamon.
2. Press evenly onto the bottom and sides of a 9-inch pie plate.
3. Brush with beaten egg.
4. Bake 12 minutes.

Filling:

1. Reduce the oven temperature to 300 °F (150 °C).
2. Whisk together eggs, egg yolks, sugars, and molasses.
3. Mix in the pumpkin puree, cinnamon, ginger, nutmeg, cloves, and salt.
4. Whisk in the cream, milk, and vanilla extract.
5. Strain and whisk in butter.
6. Pour filling into base and sprinkle cinnamon over the top.
7. Bake 45 to 60 minutes or until set.
8. To serve: Top with cream and cinnamon crunch.

Bourbon-Maple Whipped Cream:

Whip cream, vanilla, maple syrup, and bourbon until soft peaks form.

Cinnamon Pecan Parfaits with Spiced Cider and Bourbon Sauce and Maple Crème Fraiche

Serves 8

Ingredients:

1 pint (470g) pumpkin ice cream

Parfaits:

4 tablespoons unsalted butter

1/2 cup all-purpose flour

1 cup pecan halves

1/2 cup light brown sugar

1/4 teaspoon cinnamon

1/2 teaspoon ginger powder

1/4 teaspoon sea salt

2 tablespoons maple syrup

2 tablespoons crystallized ginger, finely chopped

Cider Bourbon Sauce:

5 cups apple cider

1 teaspoon ground cinnamon

5 tablespoons unsalted butter

2 tablespoons light brown sugar

3 tablespoons bourbon

Maple Ginger Crème Fraiche:

8oz (225g) crème fraiche

6 tablespoons confectioners' sugar

2 tablespoons maple syrup

2 tablespoons crystallized ginger, finely chopped

Method:

Parfaits:

1. Preheat oven to 350 °F (175 °C).

2. Mix ingredients together until crumbly.

3. Press into the bottom of a 9 inch pan.

4. Bake for 15 minutes.

5. Break up with a spoon and cook for a few more minutes until lightly browned.

6. When cool, break into small pieces.

Cider Bourbon Sauce:

1. Boil apple cider in heavy medium saucepan until reduced to 3/4 cup (approximately 45 minutes).

2. Whisk in butter, cinnamon and sugar until butter melts.

3. Boil 3-5 minutes, whisking occasionally until thickened.

4. Remove from heat and whisk in bourbon. Allow to cool to lukewarm.

Maple Ginger Crème Fraiche:

1. Whisk maple syrup and ginger into crème fraiche.

2. Gradually add confectioners' sugar, whisking continuously.

3. Refrigerate.

To serve: put a spoonful of crumbs into a glass. Top with icecream. Drizzle sauce over the top and sprinkle more crumbs. Top with a dollop of maple-ginger crème.

Vodka

Vodka is a spirit traditionally made by the distillation of fermented grains or potatoes. The neutral nature of vodka makes it perfect in baking for the purpose of bringing out flavors of the food, and aiding in the penetration of additional flavors into the dish without adding much flavor of its own. To replace with a non-alcoholic substitution, use water with a touch of lemon for tartness.

Vodka Lime Granita

Serves 6

Ingredients:

1 cup lime juice	1/4 cup sugar
1 cup water	1 teaspoon vanilla
1/4 cup vodka	1/2 cup heavy cream

Method:

1. Bring lime juice and water to a boil. Add vanilla and sugar, and stir until sugar is dissolved.

2. Remove from heat and add cream and vodka.

3. Either use your icecream maker as per manufacturer's instructions, or place in freezer, stirring vigorously every 30 minutes.

Cosmopolitan Sorbet

Serves 4

Ingredients:

2 cups sugar

2 cups water

5 1/3 cups cranberries

1/4 cup vodka

1/4 cup lime juice

2 tablespoons Cointreau

Method:

1. Bring sugar and water to a boil, stirring until sugar is dissolved.

2. Add cranberries and simmer 8 to 10 minutes. Strain, cover and refrigerate.

3. Stir in vodka, lime juice, and Cointreau.

4. Either use your icecream maker as per manufacturer's instructions, or place in freezer, stirring vigorously every 30 minutes.

<u>Vodka Choc-Orange Ricotta Cheesecake</u>

Serves 8

Ingredients:

Crust:

1 1/4 cups chocolate chip cookie crumbs

2 tablespoons unsalted butter, melted

Topping:

1/2 cup orange marmalade

1/3 cup vodka

Filling:

2 pounds (900g) ricotta cheese

1 cup granulated sugar

1/3 cup all-purpose flour

3 large eggs

2 large egg yolks

2 teaspoons vanilla extract

2 teaspoons orange zest

1/2 teaspoon salt

Method:

Crust:

1. Preheat oven to 350 °F (175 °C).

2. Mix together cookie crumbs and melted butter.

3. Press firmly into a 9 inch pan.

4. Bake for 10 to 15 minutes or until done.

Filling:

1. Beat ricotta until smooth.

2. Beat in sugar and flour.

3. Add the eggs and egg yolks one at a time until well incorporated.

4. Blend in vanilla, orange zest, and salt until just incorporated.

5. Pour filling evenly into base.

6. Bake 1 hour.

Topping:

1. Bring marmalade and vodka to a boil. Reduce to a low heat and simmer until reduced by half.

2. Let stand for 5 minutes and pour over cheesecake. Leave 15 minutes to set.

Pepper Vodka Mango Sorbet

Serves 8

Ingredients:

Sorbet:

Flesh from 4 large mangoes

2fl oz (60ml) lime juice

2fl oz (60ml) pepper vodka

1/8 teaspoon black pepper

12oz (340g) granulated sugar

Pepper Vodka:

2 tablespoons peppercorns

1 (750ml) bottle of vodka

Method:

Sorbet:

1. Process mango flesh in a food processor until smooth.

2. Add the lime juice, pepper vodka, black pepper and the sugar and process for an additional 5 to 10 secs.

3. Strain and refrigerate for 2 hours.

4. Either use your icecream maker as per manufacturer's instructions, or place in freezer, stirring vigorously every 30 minutes.

Pepper Vodka:

1. Add the peppercorns to the vodka and set in a cool dark place for 7 days. Shake gently every few days.

2. Strain through a fine mesh strainer to remove the peppercorns.

Gin

Gin, affectionately known as "mother's ruin", is a spirit traditionally made by the distillation of fermented juniper berries. In baking it pairs particularly well with lemon or lime. There are no non-alcoholic substitutions for tequila in baking, so simply skip smaller amounts, or for larger amounts, choose another dish.

Gin Granita

Serves 6

Ingredients:

3.5fl oz (100ml) water

7oz (200g) caster sugar

5oz (150ml) gin

16fl oz (500ml) tonic water

2 lemons, juiced

Method:

1. Boil water and sugar until dissolved.

2. Remove from heat and add gin, two lemons and tonic water.

3. Either use your icecream maker as per manufacturer's instructions, or place in freezer, stirring vigorously every 30 minutes.

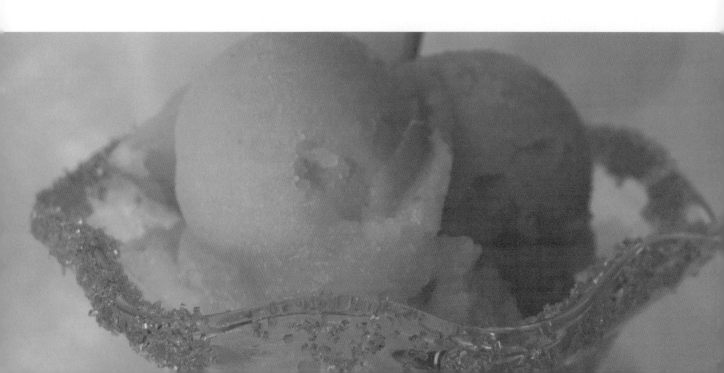

Gin and Tonic Tarts

Serves 8

Ingredients:

Base:

7oz (200g) all-purpose flour, sifted

1/4 cup of icing sugar, sifted

2.5oz (75g) unsalted butter, cubed

Zest of 1 lemon

1 egg yolk

1/4 cup tonic water

Filling:

2 eggs

5fl oz (150ml) cream

3oz (85g) caster sugar

Zest of 1 lemon

3.5fl oz (100ml)

1fl oz (30ml) gin

Syrup:

2.5oz (75g) caster sugar

4fl oz (125ml) tonic water

Zest of 1 lemon

Juice of 1 lemon

1fl oz (30ml) gin

3 juniper berries, lightly bruised

Method:

Base:
1. Blend flour and icing sugar in a food processor. Add lemon zest and butter until mixture crumbed.
2. Add the egg yolk and tonic water until the mixture starts to come together.
3. Remove from the food processor, wrap in plastic wrap and refrigerate for 30 minutes.
4. Preheat oven to 355 °F (180 °C).
5. Grease a tart tin. Roll out the pastry until roughly 5mm thick and then cut circles from the pastry that are 2 cm larger than the tart tin. 6. Line the each tart tin and trim excess. Refrigerate for 15 minutes, then bake for 10 to 15 minutes, until golden.

Filling:
1. Whisk together eggs, caster sugar, lemon zest and juice.
2. Whisk in cream and gin.
3. Pour filling into bases and bake 7 to 10 minutes, or until set.

Syrup:
1. Stir caster sugar, tonic water and lemon juice in a saucepan over a low heat until sugar is dissolved.
2. Add gin, juniper berries and zest and bring to the boil. Reduce to a simmer for 10 minutes or until slightly thickened.
3. Drizzle over tarts.

Gin, Tonic and Lime Cheesecake

Serves 8

Ingredients:

Base:
8 digestive biscuits

6 tablespoons caster sugar

3oz (85g) unsalted butter

1 shot of tonic

Filling:
14oz (400g) mascarpone

7 tablespoons icing sugar

Juice of 1 lime

Zest of 1 lime

1/2 teaspoon vanilla extract

20 fl oz (600ml) double cream

1oz (30ml) gin

Method:

1. Heat butter and sugar over a medium-low heat.

2. Remove from heat and stir in crushed biscuits.

3. Add the tonic a little at a time until slightly crumbly.

4. Press firmly into a 9 inch pan.

5. In a separate bowl, stir the mascarpone and add lime juice and part of the zest.

6. Gradually stir in gin.

7. Whip the cream until peaks form, add remaining zest.

8. Fold into the mascarpone mixture.

9. Pour filling into base, and refrigerate until set.

Blueberries in Sweet Gin Syrup

Serves 6

Ingredients:

1 cup water

3/4 cup sugar

15 juniper berries, crushed

1 rosemary sprig

2 pints blueberries

1/4 cup gin

Mint sprigs (for garnish)

Method:

1. Boil water, sugar, juniper berries, rosemary, and a pinch of salt stirring until sugar has dissolved. Reduce heat and continue to cook until reduced to about 3/4 cup.

2. Strain syrup over berries. Stir in gin.

3. Macerate until completely cooled, about 30 minutes.

Index

A

amaretto, 63, 64, 65, 66, 67, 68, 69, 70
Amarula, 6, 61, 62, 132
apple, 24, 25, 100, 101, 116, 117
apricot, 63, 86

B

Baileys, 7, 55, 60, 71, 72, 73, 74, 75
banana, 44, 67, 84, 91
beer, 4, 21, 22, 23, 24, 25, 26, 27, 28, 29
berries, 13, 14, 17, 40, 46, 49, 79, 105, 123, 125, 126, 128
    blackberry, 12
    blueberry, 14, 128
    cranberry, 120
    raspberries, 4, 16, 23, 49, 79, 106
    strawberry, 14, 21, 37, 39, 40, 46, 48, 79
brandy, 35, 76, 94, 96, 97, 98, 99, 100, 101, 102
bread, 38, 40, 41, 112
brownies, 4, 6, 13, 55

C

caramel, 56
champagne, 18, 19, 20
cheese
    cream cheese, 13, 14, 27, 32, 42, 48, 53, 54, 56, 66, 83, 93, 95, 97, 100, 104, 108
    ricotta, 121
cheesecake, 4, 5, 6, 7, 8, 9, 14, 32, 42, 48, 53, 54, 66, 83, 90, 93, 95, 97, 100, 108, 121, 127, 132
cherries, 77, 91
chilli, 105
chocolate, 11, 15, 21, 22, 23, 28, 29, 32, 33, 34, 39, 40, 44, 47, 49, 51, 52, 53, 54, 55, 57, 58, 59, 60, 62, 65, 73, 80, 81, 82, 84, 89, 91, 92, 95, 97, 105, 121
    cocoa, 13, 15, 52, 54, 58, 60, 68, 69, 90
coconut, 89, 93
coffee, 31, 33, 50, 51, 54, 57, 58, 59, 63

E

eggnog, 83, 85

F

Frangelico, 5, 30, 31, 32, 33, 34, 132

G

gin, 9, 123, 124, 125, 126, 127, 128, 132
granita, 4, 5, 9, 12, 31, 119, 124
grapefruit, 19

I

ice cream, 36, 40, 68, 84, 116

K

Kahlua, 6, 50, 51, 52, 53, 54, 55, 56, 57, 58, 59, 60, 131
kirsch, 77

L

lemon, 12, 17, 19, 24, 25, 37, 40, 41, 43, 58, 67, 78, 79, 87, 102, 118, 123, 125, 126
lime, 36, 103, 104, 106, 107, 108, 119, 120, 122, 123, 127
limoncello, 79

M

mango, 87, 122
mascarpone, 24, 25, 52, 53, 92, 127
mousse, 5, 6, 7, 8, 28, 37, 49, 73, 95, 132

N

nuts
    almonds, 44, 63, 90, 92, 131
    macadamia nuts, 73
    pecans, 27, 56, 110, 113, 116
    walnuts, 55, 84, 91, 100, 101, 102, 104

O

orange, 16, 35, 36, 40, 41, 43, 45, 47, 48, 100, 121
orange liqueur, 5, 6, 8, 35, 36, 37, 38, 39, 40, 41, 42, 43, 44, 45, 46, 47, 48, 49, 98, 99, 104, 107, 108, 120
Oreos, 31, 64

Attributions

Homemade Raspberry Sherbet by star5112

Healthy Cheesecake by Rubyran

Passionfruit Soufflé with pouring cream - wide - d'Arry's Verandah by Alpha

Chocolate Truffles by Susanne Nilsson

Amarula by rob_rob2001

Chocolate Fondue by Toby Oxborrow

Brownie Sorbet by stu_spivack

Peanut Butter Icecream by stu_spivack

Chocolate Mousse Cheesecake by Rhona-Mae Arca

Poached Pear by stu_spivack

Pecan Pie by cyclonebill

Vodka Collection by Christian Senger

Gin and Tonic by cyclonebill

Wine Glass in Focus II by James Williams

Christmas Truffles by Melissa

Meringue_8850-C by Natraj Ramangupta

Frangelico Liqueur by spyderdos

Lavender White Chocolate Cheesecake by TMAB2003

Key Lime Cheesecake by Cheryl

Brandy by Chris Pople

Orange Fruit Ice Closeup by Kim Sacha

Printed in Great Britain
by Amazon

31953019R00078